SHIPWRECKED!

SHIPWRECKED!

DIVING FOR HIDDEN TIME CAPSULES ON THE OCEAN FLOOR

MARTIN W. SANDLER

WINNER OF THE NATIONAL BOOK AWARD

ASTRA YOUNG READERS

AN IMPRINT OF ASTRA BOOKS FOR YOUNG READERS
NEW YORK

For information about permission to reproduce selections from this book,
please contact permissions@astrapublishinghouse.com.

Astra Young Readers
An imprint of Astra Books for Young Readers, a division of Astra Publishing House
astrapublishinghouse.com
Printed in Malaysia

ISBN: 978-1-6626-0204-7 (hc)
ISBN: 978-1-6626-0205-4 (eBook)
Library of Congress Control Number: 2023009227
Library of Congress Cataloging-in-Publication Data is available.

First edition

10 9 8 7 6 5 4 3 2

Design by Red Herring Design, Inc.
The text is set in Caecilia and Founders Grotesk.
The titles are set in Cut the Crap.

To Carol

CONTENTS

INTRODUCTION

Almost everything made by humans, at one time or another, has been carried over the oceans. And it's not only people and goods that depended upon the sea for transportation. Ideas, cultures, religions, technologies, and the arts historically spread by seas. "Before there were farmers or shepherds," wrote George Bass, the world's first marine archaeologist, "there were seafarers. Before people could make pottery or work metals, before they even lived in houses, they could cross expanses of open water."

At the same time, seafaring is one of the most dangerous endeavors. Some three million shipwrecks lie on the ocean floor, and along with them, much of human history hides beneath the waves. Each ship and the artifacts it carried tell a story of the people who made and used them and what life was like at the moment that vessel sank to the bottom. This makes the vast ocean floor nothing less than the world's greatest museum.

On the ocean floor, relics of civilizations that have long since disappeared lie, awaiting discovery. Unlike land sites, where the invaluable evidence of past cultures and people are often covered over or mingled with the relics of succeeding eras, an ancient shipwreck is a pristine historic time capsule. Not that long ago, most fascinating wrecks lay beyond our reach. But amazing advances in underwater discovery and excavation technology have made the finding and recovery of even the most seemingly inaccessible wrecks more possible than previously thought. At the heart of this book is another vital saga of its own, the story of how shipwreck excavations advanced from the "seek and grab" plunder techniques of the earliest salvagers to the precise and orderly science-driven excavations, leading to greater underwater discoveries and the emergence of one of the newest, most dynamic, and most rewarding of all the sciences—marine archaeology.

Throughout the following pages, you will meet an amazing array of dedicated and charismatic individuals who devote much of their lives to the seemingly impossible task of finding a specific long-sunken ship and bringing its artifacts and, in a couple of notable cases, the entire ship to the surface. These extraordinary accomplishments of not only incredible nautical and scientific achievements but also intensely personal stories of courage and determination combine to make every wreck between the covers of this book a compelling human story.

CHAPTER ONE

ANTIKYTHERA

t was the year 1900, and the world was in the midst of enormous change. In New York City, the first-ever display of the latest automobile models was about to open. In Germany, the first zeppelin had just taken flight. And for the first time in history, enormous steamships regularly crossing the world's oceans outnumbered vessels propelled by sail.

Some old ways of doing things, however, still endured. Divers harvesting sponges on the ocean floor using only a hollow reed to breathe through remained a prime industry on the Greek islands. In the fall of 1900, Captain Dimitrios Kontos and his two small sailing boats, crewed by six divers and twenty oarsmen, were making their way home to Symi after having had a highly successful summer sponging season off the coast of Tunisia. So successful, in fact, that after six months of grueling and dangerous work, the decks of two vessels were so filled with drying sponges that

This sculptured head of a Greek philosopher is typical of the quality and appeal of almost all the sculptures and statues that were aboard the ship that went down off the coast of Antikythera.

there was little room left to move about. More sponges hung down from each boat's rigging.

The two ships and their crews had left the sponging waters in mid-April and were now sailing in a channel between the Greek islands of Antikythera and Crete. This was one of the main shipping routes between the eastern and western Mediterranean, and it was also an extremely dangerous body of water, filled with shoals, sandbars, and suddenly shifting currents. Frequent storms also struck the region.

Kontos had barely entered the channel when enormous winds and towering waves began battering his ships. Driven off course, the captain sought shelter next to a rocky, barren, almost totally uninhabited small island that in ancient times had been called both Aeigilia and Cerigotto, but which now was called Antikythera. Despite the storm and the treacherous waters, Kontos, a skilled mariner, managed to guide his two boats to shelter in Antikythera's only harbor, a small cove on its northern coast called Potamos. There, the captain and the crew waited out the storm.

When the weather finally cleared and it was time to resume the journey home, one of the crew members made a suggestion. Even though the boats were fully loaded, why not dive down and see what kind of sponges grew beneath these unfamiliar waters? Immediately, one of the divers named Elias Stadiatis volunteered to be the first.

Five minutes after Stadiatis descended, he reemerged, pulling on his line, pleading to be taken back aboard. When his diving mask was removed, his face contained a look of sheer terror. He could hardly speak, but somehow he conveyed he had found not sponges but the remains of a large ship. But what he saw lying on the seabed next to the wreck plunged him into his present state. "A heap of [bodies]," he managed to blurt out. "Rotting . . . horses, green corpses."

Captain Kontos was fascinated and knew that he had to dive down himself. Dropping over the side of the vessel, he plunged himself to the ocean bottom, where he saw both the wreck and a huge mass of figures. But they weren't corpses as Stadiatis had thought: they were marble and bronze sculptures. As he glanced briefly at the magnificently crafted statues of gods, kings, and warriors and colored-glass bowls and cups, Kontos had no way of knowing he was gazing upon the largest hoard of Greek treasure that had ever been found. He could never have imagined that buried somewhere within that treasure was the most extraordinary ancient artifact ever discovered.

What he knew for certain was that he had to get back to the surface before his air ran out. Still, he had the presence of mind to do two things: First, he grabbed a bronze arm lying near one of the statues so that he would have proof of the discovery. Then,

A sculptured arm was brought to the authorities in Athens as proof of the extraordinary find that had been made off Antikythera.

he made the best mental note he could of where the wreck and the treasure lay so that he could record it once he got back on his boat.

It was now time for the party to return to Symi. It was customary for those who completed a profitable sponge-diving expedition to spend weeks, even months, celebrating their success. And Kontos and his crew did just that. But they also had a serious decision to make: What should they do about the treasure they had discovered?

One of the hundreds of sculptures, large and small, retrieved from the Antikythera wreck.

The crew decided to recover as many of the artifacts that lay beneath the waters off Antikythera as they could. They were willing to turn them all over to the Greek government if, in return, the government agreed to pay them sufficiently for each of the items and provided them with a suitable ship and necessary equipment to carry out the recovery.

Kontos enlisted the aid of Antonius Oikonomou, a professor of archaeology at the University of Athens. A fellow Symiote, Oikonomou took Kontos and Stadiatis, along with the bronze arm that had been salvaged, to meet the Greek Minister of Education, Spyridon Stais. It could not have been a more favorable time for the meeting.

The Greek government had made a public announcement calling for a concerted effort to locate and retrieve the artifacts of the ancient world so that they could be put on display. Up to this point, almost all the ancient treasures had been found on land. When Kontos and Stadiatis showed Minister Stais the bronze arm, providing evidence that the sunken ship and its treasure were at least two thousand years old, the official was convinced that an arrangement between the sponge divers and the government needed to be reached. Together they planned to make the first-ever organized excavation of a shipwreck. According to the quickly made agreement, Kontos and his men were promised full payment for the treasures they would bring up and hand over to the government. The government placed a Greek Navy ship at their disposal along with all the equipment needed to haul heavy objects such as statues from the seabed. In addition, Professor Oikonomou was named the official archaeologist of the project and assigned the task of overseeing the operation.

SPONGE DIVING

Many of the world's first shipwreck discoveries were made by people who practiced one of the oldest of all professions—sponge diving. As humble a product as it was, sponges were extremely important to those who bought them and profitable to those who harvested them. This was because of the wide variety of their uses. Along with washing our bodies, they were employed for cleaning all types of objects. In addition, they were used for applying paints and glazes, as portable drinking "cups," and as padding for helmets. Sponges were not only sold in great numbers, but they were also traded for goods or used as money.

The early sponge divers, naked and aided in their descent by the weight of a large flat stone, dove down to depths as deep as one hundred feet, where they stayed three to five minutes gathering sponges with a sharp knife and a special net. Thanks to hundreds and eventually thousands of brave divers, the sponge diving industry boomed. In the late 1860s, it got a huge boost with the introduction of a diving helmet fitted to a watertight suit. The new outfit, which allowed divers to descend to as deep as 230 feet and to stay beneath the sea longer than ever before, enabled sponge diving to be carried out on such a grand scale that thousands of divers were spending more than a million hours a year on the ocean floor.

Sadly, there was a tragic human toll attached to divers' new abilities to operate so far beneath the surface. At the time, almost nothing was known about the painful and dangerous decompression illness known as "the bends"; this occurs when bubbles form in a diver's bloodstream as a result of ascending too quickly to the surface after being deep underwater. By 1910, some twenty thousand sponge divers were permanently disabled by the bends, and another ten thousand were killed.

Despite this human disaster, the industry continued to thrive, but between the 1910s and the 1990s, developments took place that spelled the end of the glory days for sponge diving. Two world wars, between 1914 and 1945, meant that many would-be divers went off to fight and sponge harvesting came to a halt. Then in the 1980s, most of the sponges in parts of the Mediterranean and the Aegean Sea became infected with pollution. The final blow came with the development of synthetic sponges.

News of the recovery expedition made the front pages of newspapers around the world. However, because of high winds and extremely choppy seas, it wasn't until November 24, 1900, that Kontos and his men in their two small sponge boats accompanied by a Greek naval ship named the *Mykali* arrived at the shipwreck site. Anxious to get started, Kontos put his eight divers to work almost immediately. Because the wreck was located so far down on the ocean floor and because the diving equipment of the day was still so primitive, they could dive down only twice a day and remain on the bottom for no more than five minutes.

Added to their difficulties was the fact that it became immediately obvious that the *Mykali* was far too large for their purpose. As powerful as the cumbersome vessel was, it was not the easiest ship to steer, which made it dangerous to operate in such a windy site so close to shore. On November 27, the *Mykali* returned to its homeport near Athens and was replaced by the smaller, more maneuverable steam schooner *Syros*, which hurried to the wreck site in time for the divers to resume work on December 4, 1900.

Despite the fact that the winds never stopped blowing and the seas kept continuously churning, the earliest dives yielded rich rewards, including two small marble statues, an exquisite bronze head (thought at first to be that of a boxer but later determined to be that of a philosopher), and fragment after fragment of bronze marble statues. They also uncovered a bronze sword and scores of bronze bowls, clay dishes, and other pottery. It was only the beginning.

The Symi sponge divers spent the next ten months rescuing some of Greece's most beautiful artifacts, one of the greatest hoards of Greek treasure ever found. For a full three-quarters of

This large bronze sword was one of several types of ancient weapons that divers discovered and brought to the surface.

that time, the weather was so stormy that the divers were prevented from entering the sea. And aside from the weather, there was what many regarded as an even greater challenge: the Antikythera wreck was about 197 feet down. Probably no divers other than the Mediterranean sponge divers who grew up on the water and earned their living by diving could have achieved it.

By the end of 1900, the divers had recovered a large number of marble statues of men and horses, an ancient stringed musical instrument called a lyre, an enormous marble bull, another bronze sword, various pieces of bronze furniture including a throne, and a type of roof tile that had not been seen since ancient times. Now newspapers were printing daily summaries of what was

A variety of recovered Greek statues shown here in various stages of restoration.

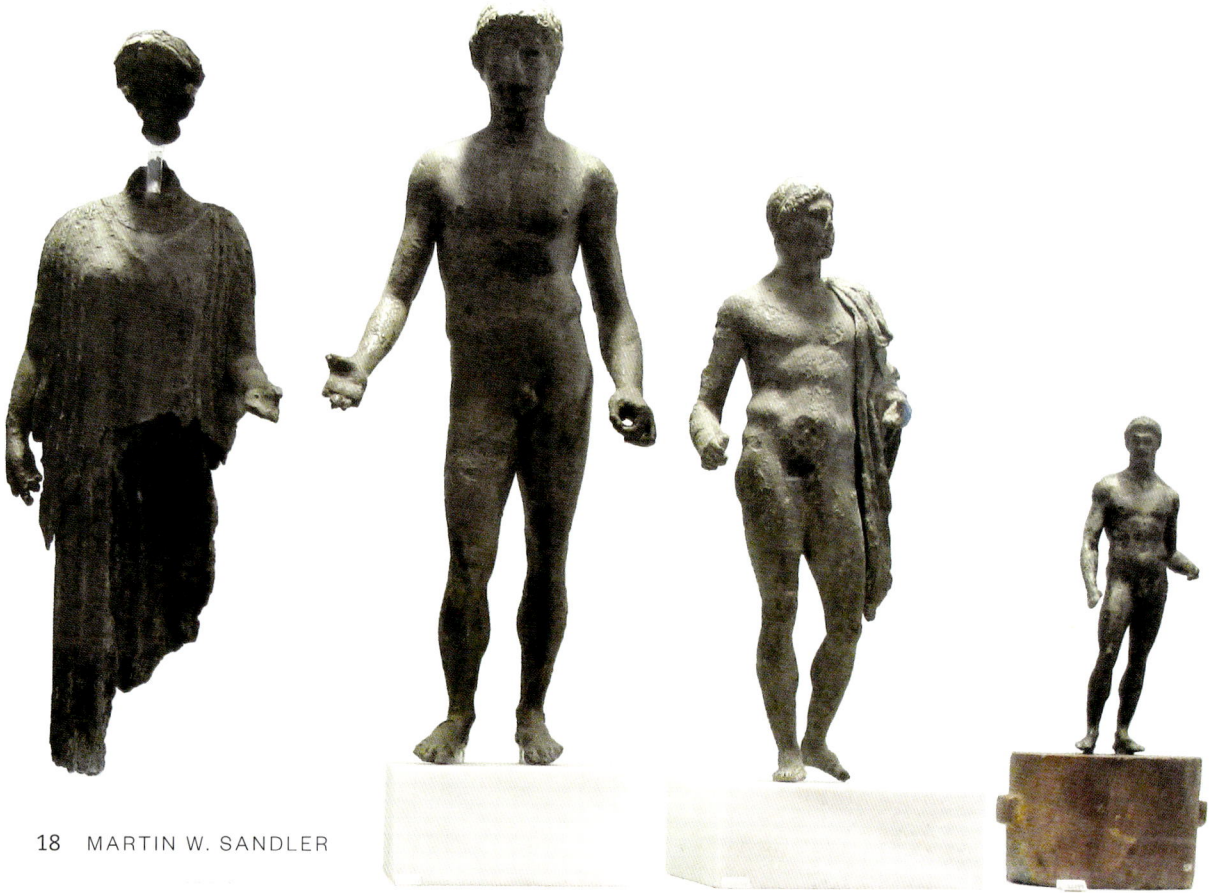

being brought to the surface. Of all the items described, none captured the public's attention as much as the huge, full bronze statue of a handsome Greek young man that immediately became known as "The Antikythera Youth." Curators at the National Archaeological Museum of Athens, where all the recovered items were taken, were also captivated by the many delicate objects that Kontos and his men were able to salvage intact. No wonder that Angeliki Simosi, the director of the Hellenic Ephorate of Underwater Antiquities, exclaimed, "The ship that sank at Antikythera was not merely a cargo ship. It was essentially a floating museum."

Then, just as the public, the curators, and the archaeologists waited anxiously to see what would be discovered next, the divers announced they had run into a serious problem. A large portion of the wreck was covered with enormous boulders, which had broken away from the cliffs that lined Antikythera's shore sometime during the two thousand years the wreck had lain on the seabed. In order to carry out further excavations, the boulders had to be removed somehow.

By this time, several archaeologists had joined the expedition and immediately ordered that the powerful naval vessel *Mykali* be brought back from Athens to aid in the removal of the boulders. The archaeologists instructed the divers to dig tunnels under the boulders and to tie strong ropes around them several times. This enormously difficult task required at least twenty divers per boulder. When it was completed, the ends of the ropes that surrounded a boulder were then attached to the *Mykali*, which, using its full power, steamed so that once in open waters, the ropes attached to the boulder could be cut away and the boulder allowed to descend harmlessly into one of the several deepwater chasms.

It was a dangerous strategy. If the ropes snapped while the *Mykali* was steaming out to sea, the shock might capsize the vessel, sturdy as it was. Even worse, if the boulder refused to become dislodged, it might drag the *Mykali* down to the bottom. As a necessary precaution, members of Kontos's crew stood by the ship with axes ready to cut the ropes if the *Mykali* started to be dragged down. Fortunately, the strategy worked. Several boulders were displaced and out of the way.

But the boulder adventure was far from over. Among the Greek officials who gathered at the wreck site to observe the progress was Minister Spyridon Stais, the man who commissioned Kontos and his crew to conduct the excavation. While the others at the scene were celebrating the removal of the boulders, Stais had a disturbing thought. What if the boulders weren't really boulders at all? What if the divers had failed to recognize that they were colossal, ancient statues that had been lying under the sea for centuries and covered with marine life?

After sending several boulders crashing to the depths far out of any human's reach, Stais ordered that, even though it presented a risk to the *Mykali*, the next boulder should be hoisted to the surface. One can only imagine the shock and then the exhilaration when it became obvious that the boulder was a huge statue of the divine Greek hero Hercules. One can also only imagine the feelings elicited by the realization that several other priceless statues had been deliberately sent to a watery grave.

The excavation continued into September 1901. By this time, significant discoveries from the wreck were becoming increasingly rare. One diver died from the bends, two others had become permanently disabled, and the rest involved in the grueling enterprise were exhausted. By the end of September 1901, the decision was made to bring the project to a halt. It had been an extraordinary endeavor, beginning with the discovery of the oldest shipwreck ever found and evolving into the first deliberate excavation of a shipwreck, work that was the prelude to what would become a brand-new science known as marine archaeology.

However, what took place at Antikythera, important as it was, was purely a salvage operation. No attempt to learn anything about the ancient sunken ship or the way of life onboard had been made. Unlike what would become the very essence of marine archaeology, none of the archaeologists at Antikythera dove down themselves to the wreck to survey the scene firsthand or record the exact location of the ship, its artifacts, and the possible locations of other buried objects. And once all that had been brought to the surface had been taken to the National Archaeological Museum of Athens, no attempt was made to identify and catalog the origin, age, or anything else about each artifact.

It was perhaps the haphazard approach to cataloging that allowed one of the most impressive artifacts to sit unnoticed—first in an open courtyard and then in a remote corner of the museum. Then, as fortune would have it, in May 1902 a museum worker brought it to the attention of archaeologist Valerios Stais, a nephew of Spyridon Stais. On first looking upon the object, Stais regarded it as nothing more than a large pile of encrusted bronze. But then, his eyes fell on two fragments in particular. One had inscriptions in ancient Greek. The other seemed to be a part of a system of interlocking gears. When he noticed the mechanized compounds of the object, Stais brought it to the attention of the museum's archaeologists. They, in turn, called in a host of experts to analyze what was revealed to be a bundle of cogwheels and dials with inscriptions.

Despite the reputations of experts who were asked to examine the device, the mystery of what it was and what it was intended to be used for was so complex that those who periodically examined it came up with conflicting theories. In 1958, Dr. Derek J. de Solla Price, a physicist and highly respected science historian, made the first truly detailed study of the object. Using a form of X-rays called radiographs, Price determined that the device contained at least twenty-seven gears—more complicated than had at first been believed. At that point, Price became the first recognized authority to officially proclaim that, remarkably, someone had created the world's first computer two thousand years ago.

Thirteen years later, and operating with the benefit of greatly advanced X-ray equipment, Price made the next breakthrough. It was now apparent, both from what Price and his assistants had been able to decipher about the device's workings thus far and from the inscriptions, that it was for looking into the future of, among other things, the movements of the sun and moon. This device would become known as the Antikythera Mechanism.

Price was not the only one devoting much of his life to attempting to solve the riddle of the mechanism. Michael T. Wright, curator of mechanical engineering at London's Science Museum, spent more than twenty years seeking a solution and in 2006 completed building a working model of how he believed the device worked.

Inscriptions aided scientists and archaeologists in unraveling the mysteries of what the Antikythera Mechanism was created to do.

Once its gears were fully uncovered and restored, it became clear that the Antikythera Mechanism was a marvel, even a miracle, of engineering.

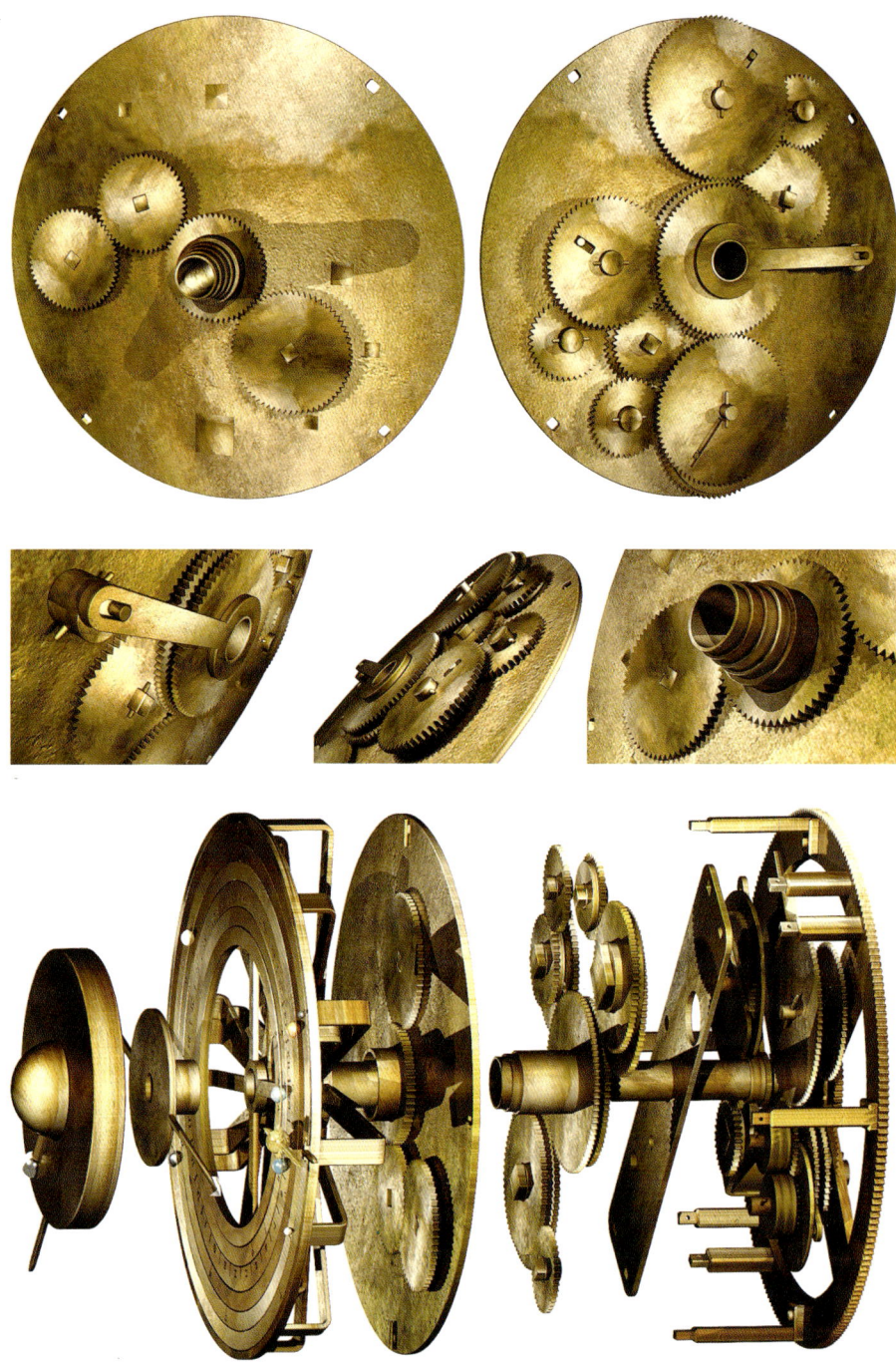

Between the years 2005 and 2008, progress toward understanding the purpose and workings of the Antikythera Mechanism took a giant leap forward when a team of scientists, science historians, astronomers, mathematicians, computer experts, script analysts, and conservation experts formed. Its members included astrophysicist Mike Edmunds, mathematician and filmmaker Tony Freeth, astronomer John Seiradakis, astrophysicist Xenophon Moussas, physicist Yanis Bitsakis, and philologist Agamemnon Tselikas.

By 2008, these researchers had collectively identified the purpose of the device, succeeded in translating 95 percent of the ancient inscriptions upon it, and had built a replica of the mechanism so advanced that no other device of comparable technological sophistication would appear anywhere in the world for at least another one thousand years after it was created.

It was a device designed and built to predict and track the position of the sun, the location and phases of the moon, lunar and solar eclipses, the movements of the planets across the sky, and even to help plan the dates of the next planned Olympic Games.

No one knows enough about Greek astronomers to be able to definitively identify the creator of the mechanism. But there is one thing archaeologists, scientists, historians, and even casual observers agree on: the astonishing gearwork is far more technologically sophisticated than anyone had expected from an artifact of this time.

The Antikythera story is an ongoing saga with no end in sight to the attempts made to discover more evidence about the ancient

Little could Captain Kontos and his sponge diving crew have realized that among the thousands of artifacts they had found would be arguably one of the greatest discoveries of the ancient world.

world. The first of these attempts was actually made in 1976 when a scuba team led by legendary underwater explorer Jacques Cousteau excavated a small area of the Antikythera wreck site and recovered hundreds of items, including statuettes, coins, and jewelry.

Then, in 2014, a much more ambitious expedition headed by Brendan Foley of the Woods Hole Oceanographic Institution and director Angeliki Simosi was armed with the most advanced underwater discovery equipment yet developed, including a new diving suit that allowed them to dive to unprecedented depths and to stay on the ocean floor for longer than had been once imagined. The new equipment also included the most sophisticated metal detectors ever invented and waterproofed iPads that enabled the team's divers to map the location of each new artifact that was discovered in real time.

During the expedition, many more stunning objects of ancient Greek art were discovered. But as interesting as these finds were,

THE EXOSUIT

The excavations of the Antikythera shipwreck, in 1900, marked the beginnings of underwater excavations carried out in what is regarded as a technologically primitive manner. Ironically, the 2014 excavations that took place in a return to the site introduced the world to one of the most sophisticated pieces of underwater exploration and recovery equipment ever developed.

The Exosuit—inspired by the space suit but with hard casing—allows divers to descend one thousand feet and to remain under the sea for up to fifty hours. Made of aluminum alloy, and, depending on its configuration, weighing between five hundred and six hundred pounds, the Exosuit is pressurized in such a manner that a wearer does not have to go through the long process of decompression when returning to the surface. Equipped with lights, cameras, thrusters, and other cutting-edge high-tech it was the discovery of a much different type of object that proved to be the most exciting find of the expedition. Toward the end of August 2014, while Foley was diving on the wreck site, one of the members of the team, Nikolas Giannoulakis, swam up to him and shouted, "We found bones! We found a skull."

While Jacques Cousteau recovered bone fragments during his 1976 Antikythera exploration, the skull was part of the most complete skeleton that had been found at the Antikythera site. As one of the world's leading DNA experts, Denmark's Dr. Hannes Schroeder stated at the time of the discovery, "Human remains have started to become a source of information that can tell us incredible things about the past. Even with a single individual, it gives us a potentially great insight into the crew. Where did they come from? Who were these people?"

Beginning with the 2014 expedition, DNA began to play an important role in understanding the origins of artifacts other than human remains. In the ceramics discovered, residues preserved

devices, the Exosuit represents a major breakthrough in marine archaeology.

Asked to describe what it's like to operate in an Exosuit, Ed O'Brien of the Woods Hole Oceanographic Institution explained, "It's kind of like riding a unicycle. . . . On your right foot, there's a pedal. Down is forward. Back is reverse. Press on your instep and it turns you counterclockwise."

Among the Exosuit's many advantages is that it can operate efficiently between two hundred and five hundred feet below the surface. (The Antikythera wreck lies at a depth of five hundred feet.) Because that's an area too deep for scuba diving and not deep enough to justify the expense of using a submersible, the Exosuit presents the first practical solution to exploring in many of the ocean's least-studied places. By the time the suit had finished making its contributions to the 2014 Antikythera excavation, archaeologists there were convinced that they had been introduced to one of the most advanced "tools" ever created to aid them in their vital and challenging work.

within them for thousands of years held DNA. "Not only are [the ceramics] beautiful in their own right, but we can extract DNA from them," Foley explained. "That could give [us] information about ancient medicines, cosmetics and perfumes."

By the time the 2014 expedition ended, divers had searched deeper within the Antikythera wreck than ever before. While the equipment was being packed away, plans were already being made for a return to the site in 2017. Foley declared, "We're down in the hold of the ship now, so all the other things that would have been carried should be down there as well. Every day is going to be like opening Tut's tomb."

In 2017, an expedition, once again under the direction of Foley and Simosi, returned to Antikythera with specific goals. One was to try and locate and possibly recover any bronze statues that might still lie hidden within or beneath the wreck. As Jens Daehner, associate curator of antiquities at the J. Paul Getty Museum, stated, "Ancient bronze sculpture in general is rare. . . . Any chance to recover more Greek sculptures in any medium, but particularly in bronze, should not be missed."

The other main goal of the 2017 expedition was to see if any other metal fragments that may have been part of the Antikythera Mechanism could be found. Using the most sophisticated underwater metal detectors ever developed, the team uncovered solid indications of the presence of at least seven statues, buried deep under the seabed. The problem is that they also lie beneath enormous boulders, which may have fallen onto the wreck during a huge earthquake that struck Antikythera in the fourth century CE. Reluctantly, Foley, Simosi, and their teams concluded that the cost of extracting these statues would be prohibitive. What they did recover was a bronze disc, which is still being studied to determine its function and whether it was part of the original Antikythera Mechanism.

From the time the Antikythera wreck was first discovered, those who have seen it firsthand have been impressed with the amount of wreckage and how large the ancient sunken vessel seems to have been. Foley has, in fact, termed the vessel "the *Titanic* of the ancient world." The most intriguing result of the explorations has been the growing suspicion that the wreckage may well represent not one but two ancient ships—and if that's the case, there are even more questions, Foley says: "Were they sailing together? Did one try to help the other?"

Whatever the answer, one thing is for certain: the Antikythera shipwreck site is of tremendous importance. As Greek archaeologist Theotokis Theodoulou proclaimed, "This is the cradle of underwater archaeology."

CHAPTER TWO

CAPE GELIDONYA

A small merchant ship, in the early thirteenth century BCE was making its way between two of the five tiny islands off Cape Gelidonya on the southwest coast of Turkey. These waters had long ago been described by the writer Pliny as "extremely dangerous to mariners," and sometime during a storm that erupted that night the vessel was thrown up against jagged rocks and plunged to a watery grave ninety feet below the surface.

In 1958, some three thousand years later, photojournalist Peter Throckmorton was completing his second summer aboard a sponge diving vessel captained by Kemal Aras. Throckmorton had gone to the southern coast of Turkey to write about sponge divers and their fascinating work. He was also interested in locating and charting ancient shipwrecks along the Turkish coast. And he was particularly curious about the wreck that Aras told

Shown here at the Cape Gelidonya campsite are George Bass (left) and Peter Throckmorton (right), two of the most important individuals in the history of marine archaeology.

him he had spotted some four years earlier. Aras had said that within the wreck he had seen a number of large copper ingots and that he had actually recovered a bronze knife. "What if those copper ingots and that bronze knife were from . . . a sea trader of the time of Odysseus and the Trojan wars?" Throckmorton wondered. "If we found a Bronze Age ship we would be like winners of the world's richest lottery."

Throckmorton was more than an experienced photojournalist: he was a skilled diver. He had not only taken courses in archaeology but also taken part in a dry-land excavation. And he had a unique conviction. He was certain that a shipwreck could be excavated with the same scientific care and precision as archaeologists working on land. In order for that to happen, he knew the undersea excavation would, for the first time in history, have to be conducted by archaeologists diving down to the wreck and not by professional or amateur divers who knew little or nothing about scientific excavation. Throckmorton had another important belief as well. "I was convinced," he stated, "that the seabed contained memories of maritime civilizations that had never been recorded. What historians had missed, the sea remembered."

In 1959, Aras took Throckmorton to the site of the Gelidonya wreck. At this point, with the search for sunken vessels still in its infancy, Throckmorton was among the world's greatest experts in dating the approximate age of a shipwreck. After diving down to the sunken vessel, he came to the conclusion it was the oldest shipwreck that had ever been discovered. He then contacted Professor Rodney Young at the University of Pennsylvania Museum of Archaeology and Anthropology and asked him if the museum would undertake an excavation of the Gelidonya shipwreck. Young agreed and recommended a highly talented graduate

student named George Bass, whom he felt would be most capable of handling the project.

Bass, whose main interest was the Mediterranean Bronze Age, was at first overwhelmed by the opportunity. "Here I am," he recalled, "sent out from [the University of Pennsylvania] never having dived before, and . . . I'm the director." He might have been a bit dumbfounded but Bass never hesitated in accepting the challenge. "Could there possibly have been any doubt!" he later wrote. "This would be the first scientific excavation to bring the precise methods of land archaeology to the bottom of the sea. And even more exciting, the excavation would be of by far the oldest shipwreck ever found."

The sponge boat *Lufti Gelil* was the launch pad from which the archaeologists conducted their thousands of dives to the Cape Gelidonya wreck site.

But before leaving for Cape Gelidonya, Bass had an important piece of business to take care of. He needed to learn how to dive. After taking six lessons at his local YMCA, Bass pronounced himself ready to take on the project.

Just before departing, Bass consulted with a number of land archaeologists whose opinions he valued. And he was not happy to hear what they had to say. Most of them told him they were absolutely convinced that archaeology beneath the sea was impossible and could never become an exact science. "Nothing much could be preserved underwater," they declared, adding that "it's not possible to execute proper archaeological plans underwater."

It was certainly not what Bass wanted to hear. But instead of being discouraged, he left for the shipwreck site determined to

This narrow strip of land served as home base for the Cape Gelidonya excavation.

GEORGE BASS

"I honestly can't help but think," George Bass once said, "I was fated to do what I do." What he did was establish himself as the father of underwater archaeology and introduce the world to an enormously rewarding scientific discipline.

Bass entered the world of archaeology several years before he headed the historic excavations at Cape Gelidonya. He received an advanced degree at the American School of Classical Studies in Athens, Greece. His previous work included helping excavate a land site at Gordion, Turkey, which, in the eighth century BCE, had been the capital of King Midas's fabled golden empire. While engaged in these diggings, he achieved his first archaeological triumph when he discovered a gold earring that dated back to King Midas's time.

In 1972, in order to both develop and promote marine archaeology, Bass founded the Institute of Nautical Archaeology, the first organization of its kind in the world. Originally located on the island of Cyprus, the Institute of Nautical Archaeology soon moved to the campus of Texas A&M, where it has flourished ever since. Led by Bass and staffed by scientists, researchers, engineers, and people from many other disciplines, the INA has been a leading force in underwater archaeology.

In carrying out their underwater discoveries and excavations, Bass and his colleagues introduced groundbreaking inventions and techniques that greatly advanced how marine archaeology is conducted. These inventions include side-scan sonar, which proved invaluable when locating shipwrecks, advanced underwater picture-taking equipment, and equally advanced methods of mapping a wreck site. Among the most spectacular of their early innovations was a plastic dome called a "telephone booth" that contained air pumped from the surface and a telephone that enabled divers at various ocean depths to enter it, remove their masks, and communicate with those aboard the dive boat on the ocean surface.

When asked to describe what were his most fabulous discoveries, Bass was anxious to convey that identifying each artifact, determining its origin, and placing it in its proper time frame is as important as the actual discovery. He stated, "I always say it's been in the library. The big discoveries are always in the library."

Along with everything else he accomplished, Bass was a prolific author and the recipient of many scientific awards. He was naturally pleased with these honors but "most of all," he stated, "I'm proud that I have played such a role in the founding of a new branch of archaeology."

Modern divers seeking additional artifacts at the wreck site have been equipped with increasingly effective equipment like the metal detector in the hands of archaeologist Claude Duthuit.

prove the "experts" wrong. "I had no inkling," he would write, "that my life was changing forever."

Challenges began as soon as Bass arrived. The camp, set up on a narrow strip of beach that ran beneath Gelidonya's high cliffs, was sweltering hot and primitive, to say the least. "No one had ever done on the seabed what we hoped to do," Bass reported. "It had been difficult to attract funding. So our camp for eight people was mostly what Peter and I scrounged from a US Air Force base near Istanbul: part of a canvas mess tent, some discarded cot mattresses, torn parachutes we strung up for shade. . . . Without refrigeration in temperatures that reached 110 degrees Fahrenheit, most mornings we lived on little more than beans, rice, tomatoes, olives, and watermelon for three months."

The conditions there may have been far from perfect, but the team assembled was world-class. Made up of archaeologists and divers from France, England, and the United States, this multinational group included Frederic Dumas, on loan from Jacques Cousteau's team of divers, and the pioneering archaeologist Honor Frost. Also on board was George Bass's wife, Ann, whom he had married shortly before leaving for Gelidonya. When asked why she tolerated the difficult conditions at the camp, Ann Bass, who would prove to be a valuable member of the team, replied, "A lot of people who have seen the beach have said they don't understand why I just didn't pick up and leave. Yes, the conditions were tough. But there was a real sense that this was something new. I got caught up in that."

It was new indeed. Unlike the Antikythera excavation, where the goal was to bring anything that could be found quickly to the surface, George Bass made it clear to everyone that this was to be the first scientific underwater excavation—the very beginning of what would come to be called marine archaeology. The one guiding

The introduction of scuba diving changed the entire nature of underwater exploration and revolutionized marine archaeology.

principle that Bass established in the first days of the expedition, Throckmorton would recall, "was that we were there to understand the site, not recover a lot of stuff. Until something on the bottom was understood in its relationship to everything else, it stayed on the bottom. Recovery could take place only when everything on the site was well recorded. . . ."

"In his quiet way," stated Throckmorton, "George Bass impressed on all hands that he was not interested in things because they were pretty, or because they were rare, valuable, or would look

SCUBA DIVING

By the time that George Bass became arguably the first archaeologist to dive down to a shipwreck, the art of diving had changed immeasurably from the method used by the sponge divers at Antikythera.

Attempts to remain beneath the sea for a significant amount of time date back to antiquity. Ancient records show that around 500 BCE a Greek soldier named Scylla used a hollow reed to breathe underwater, allowing him to remain under the surface longer and to go undetected while cutting the moorings of his enemy ships.

But it would not be until the early 1940s that a major breakthrough would allow more efficient undersea explorations, discoveries, and excavations in the form of an invention by Jacques Cousteau and Emile Gagnan. Together, they created a deluxe valve system that supplies divers with compressed air. This invention, which enabled safer and deeper dives than ever before possible, became known as the Aqualung (self-contained underwater breathing apparatus or SCUBA). Thanks to Cousteau and Gagnan, divers could explore parts of the ocean that had never been seen before, and were able to stay submerged longer than ever before to examine it.

Cousteau would enjoy a varied and legendary underwater career. He would conduct many successful undersea explorations. Cousteau became a household name when he introduced the world to ocean and shipwreck exploration through Academy Award-winning films such as *The Silent World* and highly popular television series *The Undersea World of Jacques Cousteau*. And, perhaps most important, he would forever be known as the father of scuba diving.

In the first scientifically conducted underwater excavation, George Bass, Peter Throckmorton, and others study the map that has been drawn of the Cape Gelidonya wreck site before sending divers down to the site.

well in a museum showcase; but because they were there, and they said something if only one could understand what they were trying to tell us." At the heart of the expedition was the intense planning that went on before any diving took place. "At Cape Gelidonya," Bass later explained, "as in all future excavations, we spent a lot more time discussing what we were going to do than actually doing it on the sea bottom."

In the first meticulous mapping of an ancient shipwreck on the ocean floor, one that would become a model for all future successful underwater excavations, Bass's team began by making precise measurements and detailed drawings of everything in and around the wreck.

Photographs of the entire site were also taken. Eventually, the entire area looked like a conventional land excavation with areas that needed to be explored staked out in squares, poles inserted next to spots that had been thoroughly examined, and plastic tags with numbers on them attached to all visible artifacts. Only after this was completed were tagged objects—many uncovered with the help of extremely powerful underwater vacuum cleaners called airlifts—placed in lifting baskets, raised to the surface, and taken aboard the expedition's dive boat and surface vessel, the *Lufti Gelil*. Once ashore, preliminary removal of the concretion that covered most of the artifacts from their centuries-long home on the ocean floor was begun. And it revealed an amazing array of Bronze Age objects.

The discovery that copper and tin could be combined to form a new and stronger metal, called bronze, changed the course of human history. Tools and weapons made of this extraordinary alloy began to replace those previously made of wood, stone, bone, and copper. Because bronze was so much stronger than metals previously used, shipbuilders could now construct hulls carrying more cargo than ever before. Ships were now capable of traveling farther than ever. It all led to the expansion of trade throughout the Mediterranean world.

Many of the objects recovered from the Cape Gelidonya shipwreck were brought to the surface with the aid of air-filled lifting balloons.

It also meant that the discovery of the shipwreck at Cape Gelidonya was extraordinarily important, not only because of the age of the sunken vessel and the groundbreaking way it was excavated but also because of the artifacts it yielded. In those days metals were cast into various shapes called ingots, and included in the ship's cargo were thirty-four four-handled copper ingots called oxhide ingots because they were shaped like a stretched-out oxhide. Each of them was just under two feet long and weighed about thirty pounds. They lay on the ocean floor, still stacked as they had been in the ship's hull, and next to them lay the remnants of tin ingots. It was the first time in history that the twin ingredients of bronze—copper and tin—had ever been found in close proximity to each other, on land or at the bottom of the sea.

Bringing the ingots to the surface presented a major challenge. "The first job was to free the [ingots] from the bottom," explained Peter Throckmorton. "If we could get them loose, then they could be raised. Once ashore they could be cleaned in place. It was obviously much easier to separate [the ingots] under a tent flap ashore than . . . in ninety feet of water; although if it had not been for the danger of [staying down too long] we would probably have preferred to work underwater as it was hellishly hot on that Turkish beach."

Along with the copper and tin ingots, the ship was also carrying a large number of wicker baskets filled with several hundred bronze tools, several of which had signs scratched on them indicating that they had been made in Cyprus. Included were broken parts of picks, hoes, shovels, and axes. Bass and the other archaeologists concluded the merchant captain of the ship used these broken implements as scrap bronze, which he or someone else could melt down to make brand-new tools.

Among the most interesting of all the artifacts that were recovered was a large set of sixty stone balance-pan weights used by merchants to balance their scales as they measured out the goods they sold. Also of great interest was the cushioning layer of brushwood found between thin planks of the sunken ship's hull. According to Homer's *Odyssey*, Odysseus placed the very same type of brushwood layer in a ship that he had built.

Other items recovered from the Gelidonya wreck included four scarabs (gems containing a carved image of a beetle held

sacred in the ancient Mediterranean world), a stone seal used by Near Eastern merchants to sign documents, two stone mortars, an oil lamp, a bronze razor, a cooking spit, several whetstones, and the bones of animals, fish, and fowl. Also salvaged was an astragalus, which was a knucklebone of a sheep or a goat used like a die in a game called "knucklebone." At the time of the Gelidonya wreck, people also "threw" knucklebones to receive a sign from the gods.

With each new artifact discovered, Peter Throckmorton's bond with those who sailed on that vessel more than three thousand years before strengthened. He later wrote: "One of the most moving experiences I ever had underwater was when I saw that a knot had been tied in . . . rope. The knot was a bowline, well known to sailors. It dissolved before my eyes, but for a brief moment I felt in communion with the unknown sailor who had tied it more than three thousand years ago. . . . I felt that I had seen the handiwork of a sailor who might have known Odysseus. . . . The man who taught the sailor who tied the bowline had lived . . . a thousand generations before."

As would always be the case with underwater archaeology, what was even more important than what was found was what was found *out*. For example, among the objects recovered were both a large anvil and a small anvil, two stone hammerheads commonly used in metalworking, and several stone polishers. These items, along with the baskets of broken tools and scrap bronze, strongly suggested that a metalsmith or tinkerer (probably the merchant/captain) was aboard the ship's last voyage. Further

During a properly conducted underwater excavation, as much time is spent on researching and conserving objects as there is finding them and bringing them to the surface.

evidence led to the conclusion that this captain/tinkerer/merchant would probably travel around the coasts and islands taking orders for tools and weapons. He would probably go ashore often, set up a portable foundry on the beach, and fashion the tools and weapons that had been ordered using the scrap bronze that he had onboard.

Of the greatest importance of all is the fact that what was discovered ninety feet beneath the sea at Cape Gelidonya dramatically changed ages-old archaeologists' and historians' theories and perceptions about who had dominated the trading waters of the Mediterranean during the middle to late Bronze Age. Before the Cape Gelidonya excavation took place, historians and archaeologists believed that Bronze Age Greeks known as Mycenaeans had monopolized merchant seafaring along the Mediterranean from about 1400 to 1200 BCE. After the first season's excavations, George Bass had real doubts about that. Before the next season began, he and Ann went back to the University of Pennsylvania's museum library. There they pored through every book and journal on Egyptian art and found sixteen illustrations of reliefs and tomb paintings that showed Bronze Age workers carrying ingots shaped exactly like the main cargo of the Gelidonya ship. Most important, the texts revealed that these ingots had been a gift to the Egyptian Pharaoh from Canaan (then also known as Phoenicia and today known as Syria). One painting clearly showed ingots being unloaded from a Canaanite ship.

For Bass, this evidence was supported by the fact that none of the objects recovered were Mycenaean. The scarabs, oil lamp, mortars, and seal were all Canaanite. The bronze razor was Egyptian. "Why," asked Bass, "does a Mycenaean ship have nothing but [Canaanite] weights? Why were the personal effects all [Canaanite]?

All of this pointed to the fact that whoever sailed this ship was Canaanite." To Bass, there was only one logical conclusion to what the shipwreck at Cape Gelidonya had yielded: a merchant ship from Canaan was sailing the eastern Mediterranean trading routes hundreds of years earlier than had been thought.

For historians and archaeologists, it was a groundbreaking revelation, one that would rewrite a significant part of the history of the Bronze Age. It would immediately be challenged by many experts who believed that the ship was from Mycenae, one of the major centers of Greek civilization, and would not be proven conclusive until another shipwreck was found and excavated on the eastern shore of Uluburun in Turkey some twenty-four years later.

The excavation at Cape Gelidonya was truly a landmark event. Archaeologists, instead of directing divers from the deck of a surface vessel, had dived down to the wreck themselves and had mapped, tagged, recorded, and excavated a shipwreck as scientifically and efficiently as an excavation on land. With the events at Cape Gelidonya, marine archaeology became an important scientific field of its own. *National Geographic* stated it best: what had taken place at Cape Gelidonya, it proclaimed, was like nothing "that came before it—it would literally change our notion of archaeology and the ocean forever."

CHAPTER THREE

SHINAN

Among many other revelations, the underwater discoveries at Antikythera, Cape Gelidonya, and Uluburun led to vital new information about the nature of ships and maritime trading in the ancient Mediterranean world. As late as the mid-1970s, however, there had been few discoveries that revealed the history of seafaring in Asia. That all began to change on a summer afternoon in 1975. A South Korean fisherman named Choi Hyuongyeun, while plying his trade in the deep South Korean waters of what are today known as the Shinan Islands, discovered six heavily encrusted ceramic vases entangled in his nets.

Although he was not particularly impressed with the old objects, he took them home, where they remained unnoticed for months until Choi's schoolteacher brother came to pay a visit. Spotting the vases, he chipped the encrustation off one of them

The number of ceramic, porcelain, and stoneware objects retrieved from the Shinan shipwreck is almost overwhelming, comprising the largest lode of items of their kind ever recovered.

and was convinced what he was holding in his hands was celadon, an extremely valuable East Asian stoneware characterized by its beautiful blue-green glaze.

When the brothers showed the vases to local authorities, they were told that they were obviously imitations of the real things. In fact, they said, fishermen in the area had been pulling up objects like these and giving them to their neighbors, who mostly used them to hold dog food.

Unsatisfied with the local authorities' assessment, Choi's brother took the vases to much higher authorities in the South Korean capital of Seoul, who had a much different reaction. Two similar vases were just brought to them by another fisherman who had discovered them in his nets off Shinan. All the vases were then taken to South Korea's Cultural Properties Preservation Bureau, which immediately identified them as authentic celadons from the Yuan dynasty (1271–1368), established by the legendary Mongolian leader Kublai Khan.

It did not take long for the Cultural Properties Bureau to send down divers to probe the area where the celadon vases had been accidentally hauled in. As they descended, no one had the slightest inkling that these initial inquiries would lead to what many archaeologists still believe to be the discovery of the largest treasure ship in history and the beginning of marine archaeology in Asia—particularly in East Asia.

Surprisingly, despite the lack of clues as to where exactly the wreck lay, it was found rather quickly. But at first glimpse it became obvious that the excavation of the vessel would be enormously challenging. First of all, it was more than sixty-five feet below the surface. Secondly, the tidal currents were particularly strong, continuously turning up the silt and sand of the ocean floor that made visibility almost impossible at times. Most challenging of all was the fact that there was not one person who had ever been involved in an underwater excavation in South Korea. Nor was there a single piece of any type of marine excavation equipment in the entire nation or surrounding countries.

Given the circumstances and the fact that the South Korean government was determined to bring as many artifacts from what would be named the Shinan shipwreck to the surface as possible, it was decided that divers from the Ship Salvage Unit (SSU) of the South Korean Navy would carry out the excavation while members of the Cultural Properties Administration would

The Gwangju National Museum was opened in Seoul, Korea, in 1978 to display and store artifacts and hull structures recovered from the Shinan shipwreck.

record each artifact as it was brought to the surface. As they began their work, none of these dedicated individuals had any idea that before this extraordinary excavation was over, more than nine years of effort and 7,500 hours of diving time would be required.

The long and arduous series of excavations that took place between the summers of 1976 and 1984 included 9,800 working days. They began with the installation of an enormous aluminum frame directly over the wreck of the ship itself and the wide surrounding area, which, as in the case of most shipwrecks, contained materials and objects that had been aboard the vessel when it crashed down to the ocean floor. The frame was built in the form of six-and-a-half-foot squares so that exploration of the site could take place square by square. Additional lines were attached to the frames so that even in dark waters divers could make their way and find the specific square they intended to explore.

Once the grid was installed, the first target of exploration was the ship itself. After many dives and many calculations made aboard the surface vessel, it was determined that the ship had been almost 112 feet long, some thirty-six feet wide, slightly more than thirteen feet tall, and had a cargo capacity of about two hundred tons along with the ability to carry hundreds of sailors and passengers. The examinations also provided proof that the ship had been built in China. Among this evidence were the holes that had been built into the vessel's keel, a typical feature of

Food items, including seeds and spices, were identified, labeled, and preserved.

唐船の図

假名垣
魯文暗記

唐船ハ形容頗ル美なりとハ�• 西洋の堅固なるに及ざるぞ 唐船の形容頗ル美なりとハ〔西洋の堅固なるに及〕… 〔以下縦書き漢字群〕

An early Chinese trading vessel. The discovery of the Shinan shipwreck added immeasurably to our knowledge of what was once a robust Far Eastern maritime trade.

ships made in China's Fujian province. Sailors could insert coins or bronze mirrors into these holes as part of their prayers for a safe voyage.

Once every area and every piece of the ship had been examined, reexamined, and recorded, it was time to search for artifacts, square by square. And the number, variety, and quality of the

The haenyo have become famous worldwide and have been an inspiration around the globe.

SEA WOMEN

At the time that men from the Royal South Korean Navy were bringing up artifacts from the Shinan shipwreck, another group of divers, all of them women, were operating in the area where the Chinese ship had been found. They discovered two gold bracelets that had been aboard the sunken ship. Known as haenyeo ("sea women" in Korean), these divers lived in the Korean province of Jeju.

Jeju's diving tradition dates as far back as 434 BCE, when it was an almost totally male occupation. The first accounts of women divers did not appear until the 1600s, when stories of Jeju women, some in their eighties and all capable of holding their breath for more than a minute, dove as deep as ninety-eight feet in order to harvest oysters, abalone, conch, octopus, and other foods from the ocean bottom.

By the 1700s, women divers from Jeju and surrounding islands outnumbered their male counterparts, due in great measure to the fact that so many Korean men had died during wars or deep-sea fishing accidents. The result was an enormous switch in family structure. As women increasingly became the chief money earners, they also increasingly became the heads of their families. By the 1960s, two enormous developments had taken place in Korea and its environs. Harvests brought up from the deep by the haenyeo accounted for 60 percent of Jeju's total revenue from its fisheries, and haenyeo women became the main revenue-earners in their families.

Although their numbers today are dramatically down from their peak enrollments, haenyeo remains an extremely important part of South Korean life. Girls begin their training at around the age of eleven, taught primarily by haenyeo who are over eighty years old and have been diving for some seventy years.

"[These] women," states professional diver Kimi Werner, "dive down to get food from the sea and sustain their whole community. They understand [the ocean] like the backs of their hands. What's in season, what's not in season." And, as Werner points out, there's something more. "When you are down there underwater," she explains, "harvesting by hand, it teaches you respect. You're coming home with enough to support your family, enough to support your community—and no more [than that]." Haenyeo Moon Bokhui has her own strong feelings about who she is. "I can make money, and I have freedom," she boasts. "Wherever I go, I tell people that I am haenyeo, proudly."

objects that were found were nothing less than staggering: 20,664 items made of porcelain, 28 tons of coins, 729 metal objects, 43 stone objects, 1,017 pieces of red sandalwood, and thousands of other objects including 360 information-bearing wooden tablets.

The excavation of the Shinan shipwreck produced many amazing surprises. One of the most amazing of all had to do with the hundreds of large wooden crates in which so much of the cargo-turned-artifacts was packed. Incredibly, after experiencing what must have been a devastating series of violent crashes against rocks and boulders during a more than sixty-foot drop to the ocean floor, and more than seven hundred years beneath the seas, not only were much of the contents of the crates still fully intact but so were the crates, including the wrapping string. Several of the huge boxes had the words GREAT GOOD LUCK still written upon them, while inscribed on the top of another was the pattern for the Chinese game of Go, obviously played by the sailors during the voyage.

To the archaeologists, the items inside the crates were immensely important. The items attached to the crates, however, were even more vital to the excavation's goals. Called tablets, these long wooden tags ranged from six to sixteen inches in length and up to one-and-a-half inches in width. Created before the invention of paper, a time when people wrote their messages on wood, animal skins, and other materials, these extraordinary sources of information revealed the nature and quantity of the shipped goods, the date of the shipment, and the sender's name, location, and type of business. The tags also documented the ship's point of departure, its intended route, its intended ports of call, and its final destination.

When the hundreds of tags that had sunk with the Shinan

ship were brought to the surface, archaeologists studied the information on each of them for hours on end and then shared with archaeologists, historians, and scientists from around the globe, all of whom credited this unique information with providing invaluable and unprecedented insight into maritime trade in the medieval Asian world.

For most involved in the excavation, the presence and importance of the wooden tags was unexpected. Not surprising were the celadon items that began showing up early in the operations. After all, the accidental discovery of fourteenth-century celadon

The simple-looking, so-called tablets have, in fact, in most cases, been the greatest source we have of ships' names, owners' names, the nature of cargoes, ports of debarkation and destination, and other vital information.

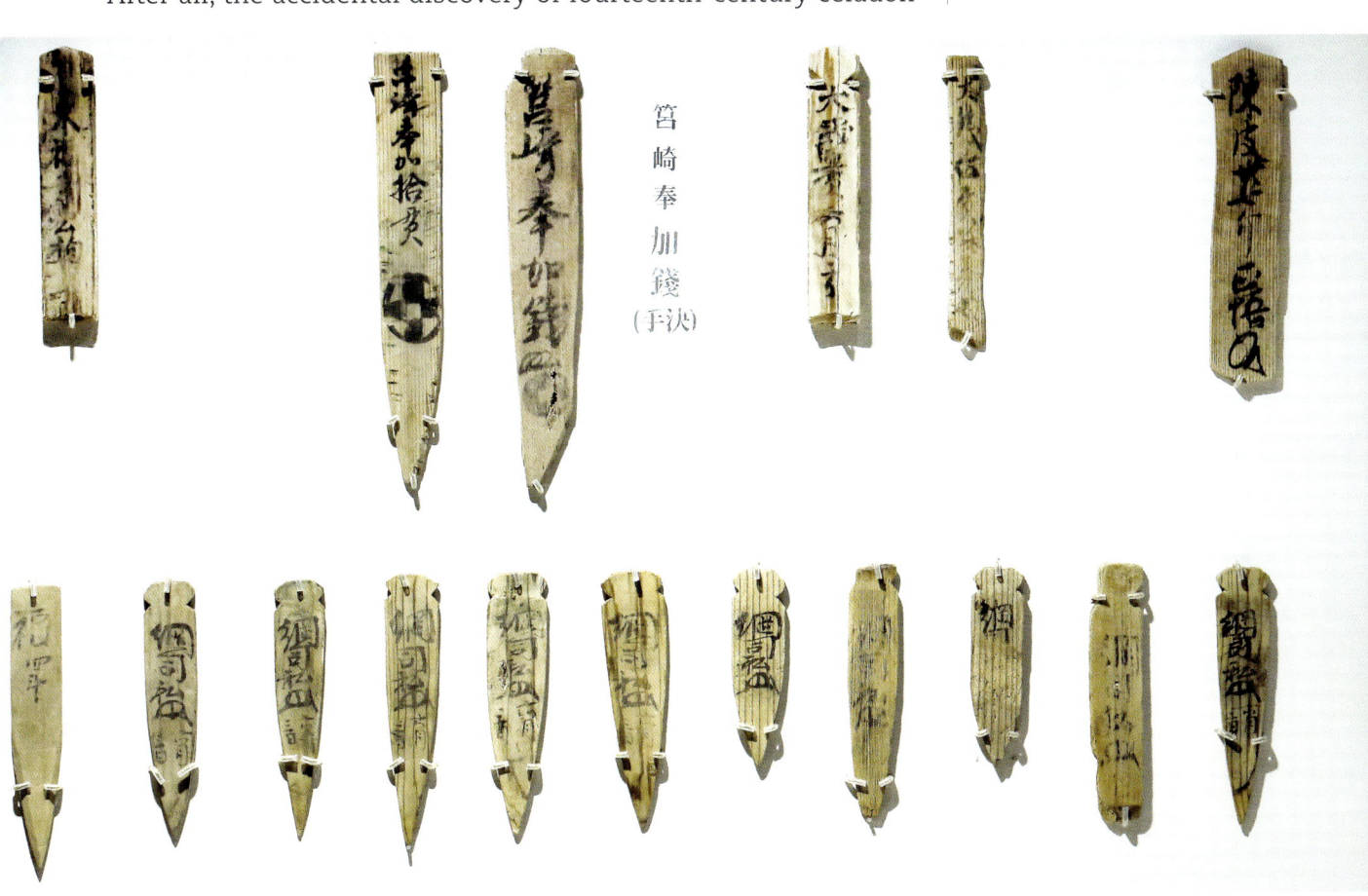

WINDOWS TO THE PAST

The twenty-eight tons of ancient coins that were a part of the Shinan ship's cargo were the largest and undoubtedly most monetarily valuable assemblage of coins ever recovered from a sunken vessel. But they were an extraordinary find for a reason other than their value.

Archaeologists have always recognized coins as among the most important of all artifacts in unlocking the secrets of the past. Coins are, in fact, so important to our knowledge of what has gone on before us that they have been called both "newspapers in metal" and "miniature libraries of history." Centuries before such things as newspapers and magazines, coins told us about leaders of various countries, what they looked like, how they dressed, and when they ruled.

The words that appear on coins are particularly important because they reveal the language that was used at the time they were created. The numbers imprinted on coins tell us about the number system used by the country that issued them and what they were worth when they were made.

Coins also add to our knowledge of the physical appearance and style of a certain place through engravings of landmarks and structures that often appear on them. For archaeologists and historians, these images are among the most valuable sources of information about architectural styles and the development of architecture over time.

Another important contribution that coins make to our historical knowledge is that by allowing us to compare currency from a particular country or region over the years we can trace conquests or upheavals in governments through changes in the official language used on their coins. In addition to all this, the quality of each coin that is found, no matter how old, tells us much about the technological capabilities of the country or society that issued it and the types of metal it could process at the time. No wonder that, along with all the other nicknames they have been given, coins are often called windows to the past.

vases led to the excavation itself. The enormous amount of celadon ware found, including dishes, vases, pictures, and a huge number of exquisite celadon figurines, the likes of which had never been seen before, was extraordinary.

Of all the cargo that the Shinan ship was carrying when it went down, probably nothing astounded the vessel's excavators as much as the more than eight million Chinese coins, almost all of which were made of metal, that were being transported to Japan to be used either as currency or in the casting of Buddha statues, which were produced in great numbers in the fourteenth century. Dates inscribed on many of the coins provided the most conclusive proof of the time in which the ship had sailed and had met with disaster.

This beautifully designed and carefully crafted object was used for burning incense.

The twenty-eight tons of coins were of immense value, and so, too, were the over one thousand rosewood logs that filled a large part of the trading vessel's hold. Used to make high-quality furniture, artworks, and statues of Buddha, rosewood (also known as mahogany) was in high demand among those who could afford it. The presence of so much rosewood aboard the Shinan ship was a strong indication that the vessel had sailed as far as Southeast Asia and with the intention of trading in Korea and Japan.

Archaeologists recorded and either photographed or drew each of the artifacts brought to the surface. The artifacts were then taken to the conservation laboratory of the Cultural Properties Preservation Bureau in Seoul, where they underwent lengthy conservation procedures. In 1978, in order to store and display

the artifacts from the Shinan ship, the South Korean government opened the Gwangju National Museum.

By the 1990s, crowds poured into the museum to marvel at the displays of artifacts from the Shinan shipwreck. By this time, the celadon objects, the twenty-eight tons of coins, and the other artifacts recovered from the ship had been evaluated by experts who had collectively determined that the first Asian shipwreck to be scientifically excavated was "the richest ancient shipwreck yet discovered."

To those who based the value of the objects salvaged from a shipwreck on their resale value, the Shinan vessel was indeed a treasure ship. For archaeologists and all others who regarded the real value of excavating shipwrecks to be something more than monetary reward, the Shinan ship was also a treasure ship. Perhaps Yi Young-hoon, the director general of the National Museum of Korea, said it best. After studying the artifacts and reading what had already been learned from them she stated, "It must have been a tragic accident, but ironically it is a treasure ship to us offering a window to the life and cultural exchanges of the time."

Along with its amazing cargo of ceramics, porcelain, and stoneware, the shipwrecked vessel was carrying over two hundred extremely valuable rosewood logs.

Archaeologists regard the human figurines recovered from the wreck as among the most beautifully crafted ever discovered.

CHAPTER FOUR

THE MARY ROSE

n 1515, the Venetian ambassador to England wrote the following description of the teenager who had just ascended to the English throne: "His Majesty, is the handsomest potentate I have ever set eyes on; above the usual height, . . . his complexion very fair and bright, with auburn hair combed straight and short, in the French fashion, and a round face so very beautiful that it would become a pretty woman, his throat being rather long and thick. He speaks French, English, and Latin, and a little Italian; he plays well on the lute and harpsichord, sings from book at sight, draws the bow with greater strength than any man in England, and jousts marvelously. Believe me, he is in every respect a most accomplished prince."

The new monarch's name was Henry VIII, and he was the latest in a line of kings and queens from the House of Tudor who ruled England from 1485 to 1603. Inheriting the throne in the midst of

Shown in all his glory is King Henry VIII, father of the British Navy.

a long period of wars between England and France, Henry was determined to finally defeat his nation's archenemy—and he intended to do so by turning England into a naval power. He began by ordering the construction of a great new warship, which he named the *Mary Rose*.

The *Mary Rose* was a four-masted ship with a hold and four main decks. It was a carrack, that type of vessel with high structures called "castles" in its bow and stern and a low expanse of decking in the middle. The vessel could hold about 200 sailors, some 185 soldiers, from 20 to 30 gunners, and a large number of specialists such as archers, trumpeters, and various officers. Ancient records reveal that in wartime the number of soldiers was doubled, swelling the number of men aboard to some seven hundred.

By the end of the 1530s, the *Mary Rose* had taken part in England's first (1512–1514) and second (1522–1525) French Wars. It had also been rebuilt twice, first in 1527 and again in 1536, when its weight was increased to seven hundred tons and its number of cannons and other weapons was dramatically increased. This addition of tonnage and weaponry was not, however, the main outcome of this second refitting. The revolutionary overhaul endowed the *Mary Rose* with the greatest naval military innovation of its time: hinged gunports. Cut into the vessel's hull at the waterline, for the first

The best depiction of the engagement in which the *Mary Rose* was sunk was drawn shortly after the battle and is called the *Cowdray Engraving.*

time in history they allowed a warship to fire broadsides at an enemy. With this innovation, the *Mary Rose* made the historic transition from a vessel that was capable of carrying guns on its deck to a warship expressly built to permanently house a battery of cannons.

On July 19, 1545, the *Mary Rose* was about to face its greatest challenge. An enormous French fleet was attempting to invade England by sailing up the Solent Strait and overpowering the British fleet and the naval facilities at Portsmouth. The French armada was not simply a huge naval force. It was the largest invasion fleet the world had ever known, made up of at least thirty thousand soldiers and approximately two hundred ships.

As the French fleet made its approach, King Henry and a huge entourage gathered in front of one of his castles on a hillside on the banks of the Solent, prepared to watch his beloved *Mary Rose* lead a successful effort to beat back the invaders. And, after waiting for a favorable wind, the flagship, commanded by Vice Admiral George Carew, sailed proudly out of its berth, prepared for battle. According to later reports, the spectators on the hillside flinched and covered their ears as the *Mary Rose* fired a broadside from its starboard side at one of the French vessels. Then the unthinkable happened.

As the *Mary Rose* turned, preparing to fire another salvo from her port side, she listed with her starboard side low in the water. Suddenly, a huge gust of wind struck the vessel, dipping her gunports below the waterline. Unbelievably, the *Mary Rose*'s gunnery crew had failed to obey an order to close the gunports

Sir George Carew was vice admiral of King Henry's fleet and lost his life in the sinking of the *Mary Rose*.

after the ship had begun to list. Tons of water poured through the openings, sending the ship to the bottom within minutes. Back on the shore, Henry VIII looked on in horror.

A large number of the some five hundred soldiers, sailors, and others who lost their lives were never even able to get off the ship. They were sad victims of another of the *Mary Rose*'s innovations— extremely strong, tall netting that surrounded the main deck, used to prevent an enemy from boarding the flagship. As many of the panicked seamen attempted to jump overboard, they landed in the netting, were unable to climb out of it, and went down with the vessel.

Despite the tragic sinking, the *Mary Rose* and its crew were the only casualties of the invasion. As the battle turned into a deadlock, it became clear that although the French ships outnumbered the English, some two hundred vessels to eighty, the English had a huge advantage. The battle took place in their home port, where supplies and reinforcements were readily available. On July 23, 1545, the French naval commander Claude d'Annebault decided to withdraw his fleet.

The loss of the *Mary Rose* and the death of so many men were a bitter blow both to the English and their king, so much so that Henry ordered an attempt be made to recover the sunken ship. Under the direction of the king's brother-in-law Charles Brandon, extremely strong cables were attached to the *Mary Rose* and then fastened to two large surface ships sailing on either side of the sunken vessel. At low tide, the cables were pulled as tight as possible. It was hoped that when the tide rose to full height and the empty ships rose with it, the ships would be able to pull the *Mary Rose* to the surface. Unfortunately, the king's vessel had settled at a sixty-degree angle and much of the *Mary Rose* was stuck deep into the silt and clay of the seabed, making it impossible for her to be lifted to the surface. Over the next few years, several other recovery attempts were made, all without success. Decade by decade, the *Mary Rose* slipped deeper and deeper into the seabed until it was almost completely forgotten.

Then, more than three hundred years later, in June 1836, brothers Charles and John Deane made a major discovery. While they were exploring shipwrecks in the Solent, particularly the 1782 warship the *Royal George*, they were asked by a group of fishermen to investigate an obstruction on the seabed upon which their nets kept getting caught. The Deanes, who had gained a measure of fame for having invented one of the earliest diving helmets, dove down and came upon the long-sunken *Mary Rose*.

Over the next four years, the Deanes salvaged a number of the ship's bronze cannons and recovered many other artifacts. At the end of that time, however, the wreck had become so covered in silt that the brothers were forced to give up their salvaging efforts and the *Mary Rose*, with its precious contents, remained undisturbed and forgotten for another 128 years.

Then in 1965, the search for the long-lost ship was resumed by a dedicated visionary and a team that he inspired to join him in his remarkable quest. His name was Alexander McKee and he was a British journalist, a historian, and an accomplished diver. He was fascinated by what lay beneath the sea. "Earth," he wrote, "was misnamed—it is a water planet. More than that, a saltwater planet. Nearly three-quarters of it is ocean and it is still unexplored. When I took up [diving] in 1958," McKee stated, "even the shallows off the local beaches were, in many cases, unknown territory never seen by man. I was then thirty-nine and the thought of this invisible, secret world lying at my feet was thrilling beyond words."

McKee was not only fascinated by the underwater world; he was obsessed with the sinkings that had taken place in the Solent. As a historian, he had studied both the explosions of the *Edgar* in 1711 and the *Boyne* in 1795. Like the Deanes so many years before him, he was particularly familiar with the 1782 capsizing of the *Royal George*, which had gone down in the Solent with more than eight hundred souls aboard her.

But it was locating the *Mary Rose* that truly motivated McKee. "Even in the local [diving club]," he wrote, "I was regarded as something of an impractical visionary. I was given to rhapsodizing on the potential of the Solent area, stressing its importance as a focal point for shipping of some sort for at least five thousand years. Many vessels, I argued, must have been wrecked and buried in the preserving mud to lie there forgotten, including the ship whose name had preoccupied me for so long."

In 1965, McKee formed an organization named Project Solent Ships to search for the *Boyne*, the *Royal George*, the *Mary Rose*, and other historic ships that had sunk in the Solent, although he made it very clear that he had no doubt that the *Mary Rose* was the "one really important wreck." "The *Mary Rose*," he wrote, "was a different proposition [from the other sunken vessels]. There were no plans of her . . . nor were there shipbuilders' models. And yet she had been the first English battleship to have gunports and to mount complete batteries of siege artillery—a really key ship in the development process at a time of rapid technological change. Virtually nothing was known about her; there was only a single authentic picture and that was not very informative. . . . No land site could offer such a vivid picture of Tudor society as it actually was."

Project Solent Ships officially began in April 1965. And McKee was far from alone in carrying it out. Thanks to his infectious enthusiasm and the lure of adventure and discovery that the project presented, he was able to recruit a small but totally dedicated group of divers and searchers that affectionately became known as "Mad Mac's Marauders."

"Dedicated" is actually an understatement. They were led by a man committed to the task. Working in tumultuous and dangerous seas in a time before the development of sophisticated underwater exploratory equipment, McKee and his men and women made an amazing 27,831 dives in their quest to find and recover the long-lost *Mary Rose*. That was equivalent to 22,710 hours spent on the ocean floor. Later, Morrie Young, one of the earliest members of the team, would recall how one of the few times he would see McKee angry was whenever someone said "if we find the ship." "Not if, WHEN," McKee would exclaim.

Beginning with George Bass and his team at Cape Gelidonya, all those who became involved in marine archaeology quickly learned that research was even more important than diving in pinpointing the exact location of a sunken vessel. McKee and his Marauders were no different. At first, the team had only what was called the *Cowdray Engraving* to give them any kind of guidance at all. A copy of the only painting depicting the sinking of the *Mary Rose*, the engraving was created sometime between 1545 and 1548. Valuable as it remains for the evidence it supplies about clothing and other aspects of everyday life during the reign of Henry VIII, and for the information it imparts through its depiction of the layout of the vital port of Portsmouth, England, in 1545, it provides little help in determining where in the Solent the *Mary Rose* went down so many years ago.

But then in the spring of 1966, a major breakthrough took place. While poring through records at the Royal Navy's Hydrographic Office, McKee came across a chart that had been drawn in 1841. On it were red crosses that showed what the chart makers believed were the locations of the sunken *Edgar*, *Royal George*, and *Mary Rose*. Centuries of shifting currents, tides, and sands were bound to have altered the exact spots indicated on the chart, but at least the team now had a legitimate clue as to where to concentrate their search.

Some six months later, another step forward took place. McKee was given the opportunity to try out newly developed bottom-searching sonar equipment. And it brought results. The equipment revealed that below the silt, where they had begun to look, there was something huge waiting to be uncovered. Could it be the *Mary Rose?* Use of this equipment bore fruit when divers came across a large object that, when brought to the surface and partially cleaned, turned out to be a type of iron gun known to have been carried on the *Mary Rose.* Then, on May 5, 1971, diver Percy Ackland made the most exciting discovery of all when he found a number of wooden frames that were unmistakably part of the *Mary Rose's* hull. The hardest work was yet to come, but at least the excavation could begin.

This cannon recovered from the *Mary Rose* shows the detail that was put into even the most lethal of weapons.

Year after year, aided by improved magnetometers that detected metal objects at deeper locations than ever before, more and more of the sunken vessel was uncovered. In 1978, a trench dug across the sunken vessel's bow revealed that two decks of the ship were still intact. Further removal of tons of silt disclosed that even after almost 450 years beneath the sea, most of the *Mary Rose* had not broken apart. It led to a major decision. Not only would McKee's Marauders recover as many artifacts as possible, but they would attempt something never accomplished before; they would try to bring the entire *Mary Rose* to the surface. By this time, McKee had turned the more than 250 volunteer Marauders into what was probably the most experienced archaeological diving team in the world.

The excavation of the *Mary Rose* yielded one of the largest and most amazing arrays of artifacts ever recovered. The more

One of the *Mary Rose*'s many bronze guns is brought to the surface and hauled aboard the excavation vessel.

than nineteen thousand recovered objects have provided invaluable insights into topics ranging from previously unknown methods of ancient naval warfare to the earliest history of musical instruments. The ship itself and the artifacts constitute a stunning time capsule, giving us a unique record of maritime and everyday life in Tudor England. Most important, the *Mary Rose* gives us insight into a Tudor warship that otherwise would be totally unavailable and, in a larger sense, provides us with an understanding of an important step in the development of the fighting ship.

Tools found among the possessions of the *Mary Rose*'s carpenter.

The various types of weaponry discovered on the sunken vessel and surrounding area have given military historians unprecedented evidence of types of large and small weapons that were not known to exist at the time the *Mary Rose* went down. Included are gun shields, a rare type of firearm consisting of a wooden shield with a small gun fixed in the middle, and small cast-iron weapons known as "hailshot pieces," to this date found only amidst the remains of the *Mary Rose*.

At a time in England when longbow archery was mandatory for all adult men, longbows, various forms of shorter bows, arrows, and other archery-related equipment were the most common weapons aboard the *Mary Rose*. More than 172 longbows and some four thousand arrows were recovered from the wreck site. The ship also carried a large supply of long poles, each of which had an extremely sharp, curved blade attached to one of its ends. They were to be used in hand-to-hand fighting that would take place if the *Mary Rose* was boarded by an enemy. A number of smoke-producing lime pots, designed to be thrown onto the

Visitors to the Mary Rose Museum study three of the ship's powerful weapons.

deck of an attacking vessel as well as to prevent the *Mary Rose* from being boarded were also salvaged. The various types of cannons brought to the surface from the wreck are particularly important to our knowledge of military history. Historians found them invaluable in expanding their knowledge of what types of large guns were aboard sixteenth-century warships.

Because they predate written records of their use and were not known to exist until after the date of the *Mary Rose*'s sinking, the navigational instruments that were excavated are also extremely important. These include the earliest dated set of European navigation instruments found thus far: compasses, protractors, calipers, sounding leads, tide calculators, and a device for calculating speed called a log reel.

What came as a complete surprise were the scores of musical instruments recovered, some of which were unknown to music historians prior to their discovery. Among these instruments were two fiddles; a bow; a shawm, which was an early predecessor to the oboe; a tabor, which was a small drum used to accompany oneself on a pipe or fife; a drumstick; and several three-hole pipes. The shawm was the earliest one of its kind ever discovered and had an extra hole for the thumb, giving it a wider musical range than later models. The tabor was also the earliest ever found and the drumstick was of a design never previously seen. These instruments would have been played both for the enjoyment of the crew and to provide them a rhythm as they raised and lowered the ship's sails. Together, the musical instruments suggest that there might well have been a band of musicians aboard the *Mary Rose*.

For many of the archaeologists and historians who continue to study the artifacts recovered from the *Mary Rose*, the most exciting of all are the items of clothing, the remnants of games and books, the bowls and tankards—in other words, the personal possessions that reveal so much about what life was like in sixteenth-century Tudor England.

Perhaps the most revealing of all the artifacts are the remains of so many of those who were aboard the ill-fated ship. The bones of 179 people were found during the *Mary Rose*'s excavation. Unlike almost any other underwater endeavor of its kind, 92 nearly full skeletons associated with specific individuals were assembled. Comprehensive study has revealed that the *Mary Rose*'s crew was all male and that more than 80 percent of the crew was under thirty years of age, some between eleven and thirteen years old. The studies also disclosed that many had a medical condition called "os acromiale," which affected their shoulder blades, an affliction brought about by stress that occurs on the arm and shoulder muscles when shooting an arrow. The obvious conclusion was that many of these men were archers. Further analysis of the skeletons revealed that many of these crew members had suffered from such ailments as malnutrition, rickets, and scurvy, conditions commonly associated with those who spent most of their time working on early merchant or naval vessels.

As is the case with almost all archaeological endeavors, the

A tankard from the *Mary Rose* (top)

One of the *Mary Rose*'s many lanterns (bottom)

The fact that the crew of the *Mary Rose* all died within minutes of each other makes the human remains found at the wreck site particularly important because they present us with a cross section of a community at one specific moment in time.

The biggest surprise to emerge from the detailed studies of the remains was the revelation that the previously held belief that Tudor England was an all-white, native-born population was simply not true. The number of objects recovered from the *Mary Rose* suggests that some of the crew were from outside England. Alexzandra Hildred, the head of research and curator of human remains at the Mary Rose Trust stated, "We never expected this diversity to be so rich."

The analysis of the remains, conducted by researchers from Cardiff University, the Mary Rose Trust, and the British Geological Survey, were among the most extensive ever undertaken. Focusing on the remains of eight crew members, whose skeletons were almost fully or nearly fully complete, the researchers used a technique called multi-isotope analysis on teeth to determine where these eight individuals had come from and where they had lived during their early years.

A man identified as the ship's Archer Royal, whose skeleton was found under a cannon on the *Mary Rose*'s main deck, was revealed to have been born and spent his early years in North Africa, miles away from the coast. Isotope analysis of the man previously identified as one of the ship's carpenters not only confirmed his role on the *Mary Rose* but also revealed that he came to England from Spain, a possibility that had been previously suggested by the Spanish-style tools found in a chest containing items that strongly indicated this was his cabin. One of the biggest riddles presented by the remains had concerned the origins of the man whose elegant clothing found in his cabin had led to him being referred to as the "Gentleman." Here too, isotope analysis of his teeth solved the mystery, determining conclusively that his roots were not in England but in Italy.

For young visitors to the *Mary Rose*, one of the most interesting results of the detailed analysis of the skeletons and bones has to do with the ship's dog, whom the researchers have named Hatch. "Originally thought to be an officer's lapdog," writes one of the *Mary Rose* Museum's curators, "we now believe that he was the ship's ratter, hunting rats in the hold. While some rats were found on the *Mary Rose*, they're few enough for us to believe that Hatch did a good job!"

search for artifacts from the *Mary Rose*, successful as it was, also had its share of disappointments. All the divers and archaeologists, for example, got especially excited when a chest containing a secret compartment was brought up to the surface. What particularly valuable or revealing treasure could be hidden within it? "It was like a time capsule within a time capsule," says archaeologist Christopher Dobbs. "But it only had a pin in it. Maybe this once was used to hold together some important papers that have not survived. We will never know."

What we do know is that aside from the thrill of discovery that the recovery of each artifact brought with it, the raising of the *Mary Rose* was an extraordinary adventure. It began in late 1981 when McKee and his Marauders were confident they had excavated most of the artifacts. There was a carefully conceived plan in place for the raising of the ship. But then a pre-raising inspection of the sunken vessel revealed that most of the nails in the planks inside the ship had corroded during the more than four hundred years it had been submerged. That meant the nails were bound to come loose during the raising, causing the loss of many of the timbers and untold damage to the hull. There was only one solution. The internal structure of the ship would have to be dismantled before the raising could begin. Each plank would have to be numbered, recorded, and placed carefully on the seabed so that it

One of the greatest accomplishments of the restorers, conservators, and other experts at the Mary Rose Museum has been their ability to use human remains found at the wreck site to dramatically and accurately show us what several members of the crew looked like.

HOWARD DORIS

could be returned to its proper position once the restoration of the *Mary Rose* in the dry dock began.

It was a long process. It wasn't until June 1982 that it was completed and the raising could begin. The first step was the laborious process of completely surrounding the hull of the *Mary Rose* with a 117-foot-long and 49-foot-wide steel framework. That accomplished, an enormous cradle, as big as a large ship, was lowered to the seabed and placed next to the *Mary Rose*. The plan then called for a mammoth floating crane, as tall as one of England's largest cathedrals, to hook into the framework and raise it upward and sideways to a position directly above the cradle. Then the hull would be lowered into the cradle and the crane would slowly lift the 580-ton package of hull, framework, and cradle to the surface.

It was an enormous and risky undertaking—one that had never been tried before. Would it work? On October 11, 1982, a huge crowd of reporters, journalists, and people from all walks of life stood on the dock of the Portsmouth Naval Base gazing anxiously out to the open sea beyond the entrance to Portsmouth Harbor. In addition, more than sixty million people around the world sat glued to their television sets staring at the same scene. Then suddenly the sea erupted and to the amazement and delight of the vast audience, the *Mary Rose* appeared above the water for the first time since the reign of Henry VIII.

The *Mary Rose* sits in the cradle in which she made her last journey where all could see her once again.

As soon as the ship was fully above the surface, huge pumps were used to remove the water within her. Then, the once-pride of the British Navy was placed on a huge barge for the short journey into the harbor and to the dry dock. But not without incident! As the *Mary Rose* was being lifted onto the barge a heavy cable gave way causing a loud and frightening noise. "An unforgettable crunch was heard. . . ," recalled Margaret Rule, the archaeological director of the search project. "All hearts stopped but no damage had been done to the ship. The lift continued and by [dinnertime], the whole package was safely on the barge."

After undergoing more that thirty-one years of constant and various forms of conservation, the *Mary Rose* sits in her special viewing dock at the Mary Rose Museum.

CONSERVING THE *MARY ROSE*

As is the case with all excavated shipwrecks, the story of the *Mary Rose* does not end with its recovery from the ocean floor. Far from it. Whether it was made of wood, metal, glass, leather, or fabric, every one of the more than 19,000 artifacts had to undergo conservation treatment once it was brought to the surface— and no single conservation treatment was right for all objects; each one required its own unique approach.

The much more difficult and much longer job had to do with the *Mary Rose* herself. As soon as the historic vessel was lifted out of the ocean floor sediment that had protected her for more than 450 years, the ship's timbers began to be attacked by fungi and bacteria and to react negatively with oxygen. What followed was one of the longest conservation projects on an entire ship ever undertaken. For twelve full years, the *Mary Rose*'s timbers were sprayed with water. Then, for another nineteen years it was sprayed with a preservative called polyethylene glycol (PEG). When that process was completed, the ship was slowly air-dried to remove any remaining moisture that had saturated the wood after having been immersed in seawater for so long. When it was finally completed, the conservation of the *Mary Rose* took much longer than the total amount of time that the ship had spent serving her king and country.

As the barge and its accompanying fleet of vessels then made their way toward the harbor, Wendell Lewis, director of the recovery operation, sent a message to the top harbor official. "Request permission," it stated, "for *Mary Rose* to re-enter Portsmouth Harbor after a rather long commission of 437 years." Permission was quickly granted and King Henry's favorite ship was home again at last.

CHAPTER FIVE

SÃO JOSÉ PAQUETE DE AFRICA

Sometimes sunken vessels can go beyond revealing what has gone on before; they can cause us to reflect seriously upon what has been lost, strayed, or stolen in our history and can motivate us to take steps to rectify the situation. There is no better example of this than the story of the ship formally known as the *São José Paquete de Africa*. It begins on April 27, 1794, when a ship named the *São José Paquete de Africa*, owned by Antonio Perreira and captained by his brother Manuel, set sail from Lisbon, Portugal, and headed to Mozambique, Africa, with 1,400 valuable iron bars aboard. The *São José* was engaged in the evilest of all enterprises: slave trading. When it reached Mozambique, the majority of the bars, along with wine, gunpowder, olive oil, and dry goods, were used to purchase between 400 and 500 people. On December 3, 1794, with the enslaved people shackled

Today, various individuals and dedicated groups, like Diving with a Purpose, continue to search for important artifacts from the *São José Paquete de Africa* wreck.

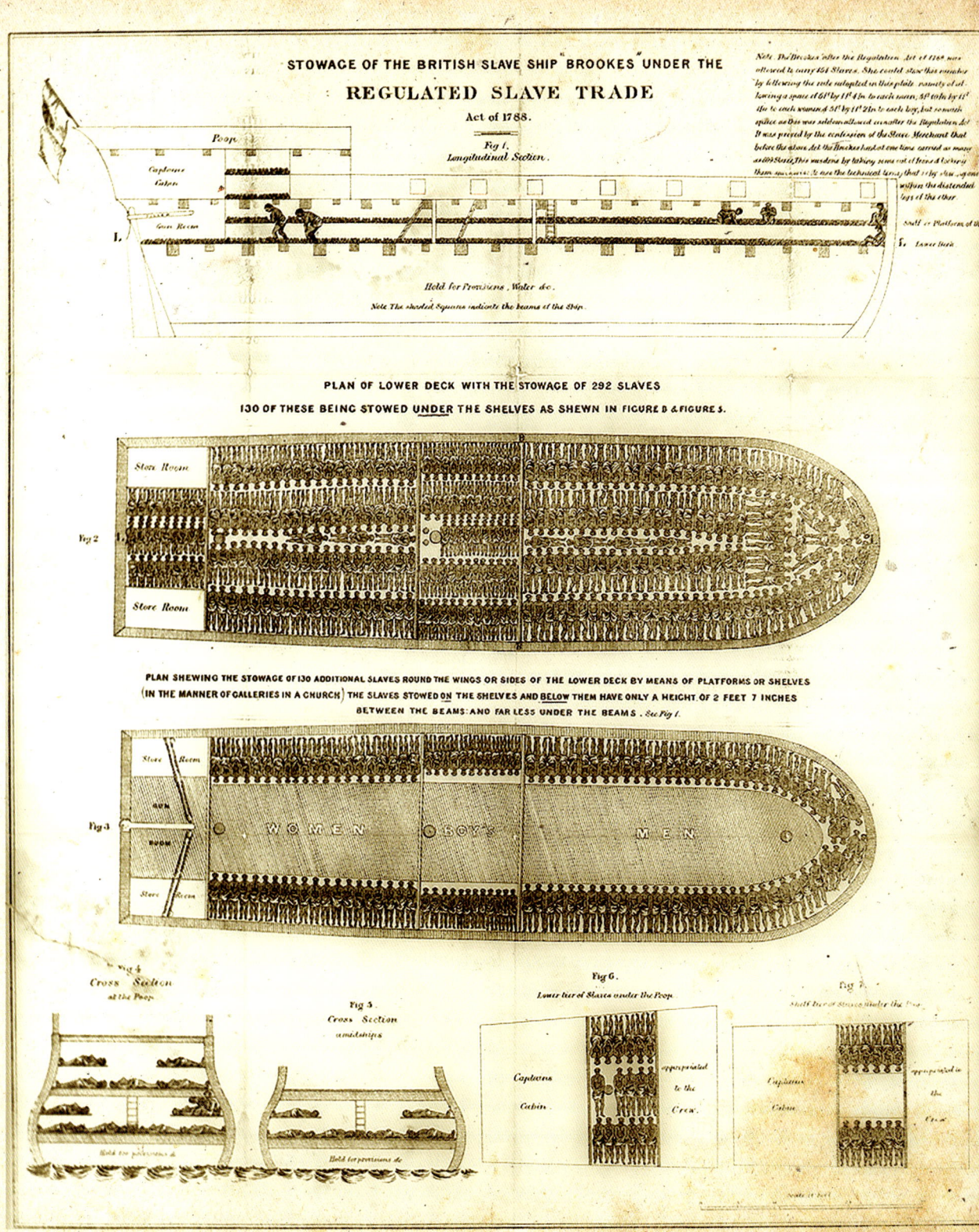

STOWAGE OF THE BRITISH SLAVE SHIP "BROOKES" UNDER THE

REGULATED SLAVE TRADE

Act of 1788.

Fig 1.
Longitudinal Section.

Poop

Hold for Provisions, Water &c.
Note. The shaded Squares indicate the beams of the Ship.

PLAN OF LOWER DECK WITH THE STOWAGE OF 292 SLAVES

130 OF THESE BEING STOWED UNDER THE SHELVES AS SHEWN IN FIGURE 0 & FIGURE 5.

Store Room

Fig 2

Store Room

PLAN SHEWING THE STOWAGE OF 130 ADDITIONAL SLAVES ROUND THE WINGS OR SIDES OF THE LOWER DECK BY MEANS OF PLATFORMS OR SHELVES
(IN THE MANNER OF GALLERIES IN A CHURCH) THE SLAVES STOWED ON THE SHELVES AND BELOW THEM HAVE ONLY A HEIGHT OF 2 FEET 7 INCHES
BETWEEN THE BEAMS: AND FAR LESS UNDER THE BEAMS. See Fig 1.

Store Room

GUN
ROOM

Fig 3

Store Room

WOMEN   BOYS   MEN

Fig 4.
Cross Section
at the Poop.

Fig 5.
Cross Section
amidships

Fig 6.
Lower tier of Slaves under the Poop.

Captains
Cabin

appropriated
to the
Crew.

Captains
Cabin

appropriated in
the
Crew.

Hold for provisions &c.

Hold for provisions &c.

and crammed into the vessel's hold, the *São José* took to the seas again and headed for Maranhão, Brazil, where its human cargo would be traded for sugar, tobacco, cotton, and other products.

Although the slave trade—particularly the taking of African people to the Americas, where they would be forced to work—was centuries old, the voyage of the *São José* signaled a new era in the practice. Up to this point, the vast majority of enslaved people taken to the Americas had been captured in West Africa. But by the 1790s, anti-slave patrols, mainly from England, intent on putting an end to slavery, had so increased in number in West African waters that those involved in the slave trade turned their attention to East African countries like Mozambique. The *São José* was one of the very first ships to attempt the much longer 7,000-mile voyage from East Africa to Brazil.

It was expected that the *São José*'s voyage would take some four months. Instead, it lasted only a few weeks. Early in the morning of December 27, 1794, as the ship was rounding the Cape of Good Hope and nearing Cape Town, where it intended to take on supplies, it was struck by the violent winds and tumultuous seas that characterized the area. Thrown completely off course, the *São José*, dragging its anchor, was thrown up onto huge rocks and began to splinter apart. Acting quickly, Captain Perreira tried to haul the ship off the rocks by using another anchor, but its rope broke. Then he sent a small boat toward the shore carrying a rescue line, but that boat was also captured by the wind and the seas and destroyed.

Meanwhile, residents of Cape Town who had witnessed what had taken place succeeded in sending a rescue line from the shore to the ship. Although both the air and the water were freezing, Captain Perreira, his entire crew, and some of the enslaved people

A page from a nineteenth-century book shows how the largest number of captives possible were crammed aboard ships.

made it to safety. But 212 of the captives drowned as the *São José* sank beneath the waves. The enslaved people who had miraculously made it to shore had not, however, found freedom. Within days, they were sold to local buyers and entered a whole new phase of life in bondage.

As for the *São José*, for almost two hundred years the sunken ship lay undiscovered in deep water only sixty yards from shore. Then, in the 1980s, local divers stumbled upon it but misidentified it as a Dutch merchant ship. In 2011, however, marine archaeologist Jaco Boshoff entered the picture. Boshoff was one of the founders of an organization called the Slave Wrecks Project (SWP), whose mission is to understand the slave trade through the discovery and archaeological study of shipwrecks.

A collaboration between archaeologists, historians, and researchers from the Iziko Museums of South Africa, George Washington University, the United States Park Service, the African Centre for Heritage Activities, the Smithsonian National Museum of African American History and Culture, and the organization Diving with a Purpose, the formation of such a group was long overdue. As marine archaeologist and Boshoff's co-SWP founder Stephen Lubkemann has stated, "There had been more studies of [ships] in bogs in Ireland at that time and . . . Civil War ships, and Viking ships. The neglect of this made no sense. There was a huge gap in our field."

As part of his attempt to fill in this gap, Boshoff was conducting research in the South African National Archives in Capetown when he discovered the *São José*'s captain's long-neglected written testimony describing, among other things, the location of the vessel's sinking. Also contained in his report was Captain Perreira's description of the bars that the vessel was carrying as ballast to

Cape Town, from Table Bay

keep the ship steady while transporting such a large human cargo to Brazil.

The discovery of the historic document led to further research in Europe, Brazil, and Mozambique in search of facts about the *São José* and its ill-fated voyage. In 2011, armed with all that had been uncovered, Boshoff, Lubkemann, and other SWP members dove down to where the wreckage of the *São José* was scattered. When they came upon the iron bars and the distinctive copper sheathing that was also mentioned in the documents they had studied, they knew they had found the *São José*. This marked the first known discovery of a ship that had sunk while transporting enslaved people.

In 1794, Cape Town harbor, the site of the sinking of the *São José Paquete de Africa*, was one of the most picturesque harbors in the world.

SÃO JOSÉ PAQUETE DE AFRICA

THE MIDDLE PASSAGE

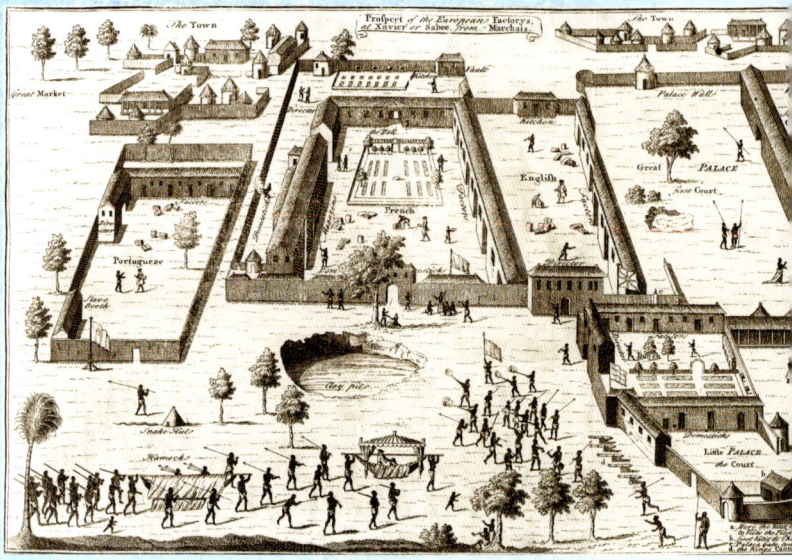

The heavily guarded places on the African coast where enslaved people were held awaiting ships to take them in bondage to New World plantations were called slave factories.

The Middle Passage refers to the forced voyage of people from Africa to the Americas, where they would be made to work in horrendous conditions and held in bondage for the rest of their lives. Before boarding the ships, many had been imprisoned for months in "slave factories," where people who had been captured either by European settlers or rival African kingdoms or tribes were held until they were sold or traded for goods. Of the more than twenty million who were taken captive, at least half died on the ghastly march to the "factories" that were scattered mainly along Africa's west coast.

Once forced aboard the ships, the enslaved people were restrained with shackles and branded with hot irons. They were packed together so tightly that as one crewman recalled, "There was not room to put down the point of [a] stick between one and another." Many had no idea, exactly, what was happening to them. Olaudah Equiano, who had been captured as a boy, later wrote about his experiences. "When I looked round the ship too and saw a large furnace of copper boiling, and a multitude of black people of every description chained together, every one of their countenances expressing dejection

and sorrow, I no longer doubted of my fate and quite overpowered with horror and anguish, I fell motionless on the deck and fainted," Equiano recalled. "I asked if we were not to be eaten by those white men with horrible looks, red faces, and long hair?"

Despite the odds, many captives tried to free themselves, and there were a number of revolts, particularly when the vessel was anchored on the African coast. But given how heavily armed the crew was, these endeavors were bound to fail.

From the sixteenth to the nineteenth centuries, approximately twelve million Africans were transported across the Atlantic as human property. The era when the *São José* set sail, 1560 to 1850, more than 4.8 million people were forcibly taken to Brazil. It will never be accurately known how many people were kidnapped via the Middle Passage and sold into slavery.

The recovery of the artifacts in and around the wreck of the *São José* has, from the beginning, been challenging to say the least. As on the day the ship sank, after it had been thrown against the rocks, the waters in which the shattered vessel lies are cold and unpredictable. Storms in the area are both frequent and dangerous. The currents that sweep in from Antarctica are so powerful they sometimes create waves that are three feet high. "It's like diving into a washing machine," Stephen Lubkemann has said. "This is one of the hardest sites I've ever worked." Dr. Paul Gardullo, historian and curator at the Smithsonian's National Museum of African American History and Culture, one of the collaborating partners of the Slave Wrecks Project, agrees that the tumultuous waters that surround the *São José* shipwreck site have made excavation terribly difficult. "'It's a pretty intense site,'" he says. "'Because of the tides there and the surge, there's a continual churning of the water.'" With such unpredictable water conditions, researchers have difficulties not only properly recording where each object has been discovered, but also physically removing the objects.

According to Gardullo, there is an important positive side to these challenges as well. "'That constant churning of the sand that broke apart the ship also may have helped to protect some of the pieces of it.'" After the sand is vacuumed off, he explains, "'within a few hours, the sand has re-covered the site, and within a day or so, there'll be two to three feet of sand back over the site.'" Gardullo emphasizes that it's the sand that has protected the artifacts "'that would have otherwise been lost to history.'"

Given the fact that artifacts from the *São José* shipwreck are widely scattered on the ocean floor and that the shifting sands and silt on the ocean floor will continue to cover each of the

Among the most disturbing objects found during the excavation of the *São José* were shackles used to hold people practically motionless during the long and devastating voyage.

SÃO JOSÉ PAQUETE DE AFRICA

remaining objects, the excavation of the vessel will, without doubt, go on for years. Those artifacts that have been recovered have, since their excavation, been on display at the Smithsonian Institution's National Museum of African American History and Culture. The museum's founding director, Lonnie G. Bunch III has said he believes that the exhibition will undoubtedly help Americans "do something they don't do well," which is to reckon with the legacy of slavery in American history.

Of the several types of artifacts that have thus far been recovered from the vessel, two of the most notable have been the iron bars

Because of its historic importance, underwater searches for evidence off the *São José* shipwreck continue today.

DIVING WITH A PURPOSE

One of the groups engaged in recovering and recording the remains of the *São José Paquete de Africa* was an American nonprofit organization called Diving with a Purpose (DWP), whose main goal is locating and documenting shipwrecks related to the Atlantic slave trade. Founded in 2003 by divers from the National Association of Black Scuba Divers, most notably Ken Stewart, Dr. Albert José Jones, and Jay Haigler, DWP has participated in the recovery of relics from slave ships in Africa, Brazil, Cuba, and the United States.

Jay Haigler states, "When we are documenting ships involved in the global slave trade, this is consecrated ground. We are investigating the greatest crime ever against humanity. . . . The important thing is to make sure the story is told." DWP member Alannah Vellacott, a marine ecologist with almost twenty years of diving experience, believes that Black divers have a special interest in telling the often-neglected story of the slave trade by personally conducting the underwater archaeological work. "No one is going to tell our history for us—not truthfully, not without white saviours," she has stated. "A lot of our history lies beneath the waves. If we do not retrieve our history ourselves, it will be 'discovered' and downplayed or be disregarded and continue to dissolve into nothing."

For Vellacott, coming into contact with the wreck of a slave ship is an intensely personal experience. Recalling the first time she dived down to a sunken slave vessel, she remembered, "It was almost like you could hear screaming. I generally love scuba diving. I feel at home, I feel at peace. But [on this dive] my heart was racing the entire time. It was almost like I was meeting face to face with a relative who I'd never known, whose story was never told, and they really wanted to share something with me. It was very, very moving."

Vellacott's sentiments are shared by Dr. Albert José Jones, one of the world's most experienced divers. "I've seen grown men— big 250-pound guys with a bunch of muscles— tough guys break down and cry," he says. "Especially when we find something like the shackles that were made for children. This is a lot different. This is more than just fun and going down taking pictures. This has to do with digging up history, filling in the gaps. I've had the opportunity to see artifacts that have come up from the slave wrecks. I had the chance to go out and dive the wrecks. And it was not like any other dive. It was like touching the souls of your ancestors."

SÃO JOSÉ PAQUETE DE AFRICA

and the distinctive copper fastenings that helped identify the sunken ship in the first place. Eliciting the most emotional responses from those who have seen the artifacts are the iron shackles, particularly several designed for children.

The discovery of the *São José* was an extraordinarily important event, not only for its discovery itself but for what it means to the world. As Boshoff has stated, "The story of the *São José* is the story of just one ship, but it is like thousands of other voyages. Ultimately, the *São José* compels us to confront and remember the brutal practice of the slave trade and to acknowledge its role in shaping the world in which we live." It is a compulsion that is deeply felt by those like Gardullo. "Our work," he says, "is bigger than just a search for shipwrecks. It is about . . . the way we talk about the slave trade and its connection to our world and ourselves."

This awareness of a "connection to the world" has perhaps been the most surprising outcome of the first discovery and excavation of a slave-carrying vessel. Justice Albert Louis Sachs, one of the writers of South Africa's first democratic constitution, is a resident of Clifton, South Africa, the Cape Town beach community off which the *São José* sank. Justice Sachs sees the remains of a slave ship lying so close to such a beautiful spot as a reminder of the dark side of history. "And it's not just our history," he states, "it's the history of the world." Impressed with the way in which the finding of the *São José* has led to the search for other slave ships, he says, "I think the value of these kind of discoveries is that they are being undertaken by people from all over the world . . . in a concerted international effort to understand, and reveal, and respond to, and even take a kind of responsibility for, what was an international form of depravity."

CHAPTER SIX

THE HUNLEY

Throughout history, some of the most sought-after shipwrecks have been those that played an important role in the nation's history before meeting an unfortunate end. One of these wrecks was the Confederate Civil War vessel the *H. L. Hunley*, the first submarine to sink an enemy vessel in combat.

Named for its inventor and funder Horace Lawson Hunley, it was built in Mobile, Alabama, and launched in July 1863. Compared to today's submarines, it could not have been more primitive. Constructed out of a forty-foot-long cylindrical steam boiler, the *Hunley* was designed for an eight-man crew—seven to turn the hand-cranked propeller and a commander to control the steering and the depth. It also had two watertight hatches for entering and leaving the vessel, one at the front and another at the rear, and two short conning towers equipped with small portholes.

In this painting, H. L. Hunley, the creator of the submarine bearing his name, stands accompanied by a guard assigned to protect the vessel.

The *Hunley* was originally designed to attack a ship using a torpedo-like explosive floating device that was towed at the end of a long rope. The sub was to approach an enemy ship on the surface, then dive under her, and surface again beyond her on the other side. The "torpedo" would be drawn against the ship and explode.

This plan, however, was abandoned. It was considered too dangerous because of the possibility of the towline becoming tangled in the *Hunley*'s propeller, or because the "torpedo" could drift and slam into the *Hunley* instead of the enemy vessel. Instead, a twenty-two-foot pole was affixed to the submarine's bow. At the end of the pole sailors affixed a copper cylinder containing 135 pounds of black powder designed to explode on contact as it was pushed against the hull of a ship at close range.

On August 12, 1863, after having completed trial runs in Mobile Bay, the *Hunley* was transported by rail to Charleston, South Carolina. There, Horace Hunley and his partners intended to operate the submarine as a privateer, helping the Confederacy break the blockade the North had placed on Southern ports. But as soon as

This diagram shows how the *Hunley* was propelled by the crew with each man positioned at a designated spot where he turned the propelling crank.

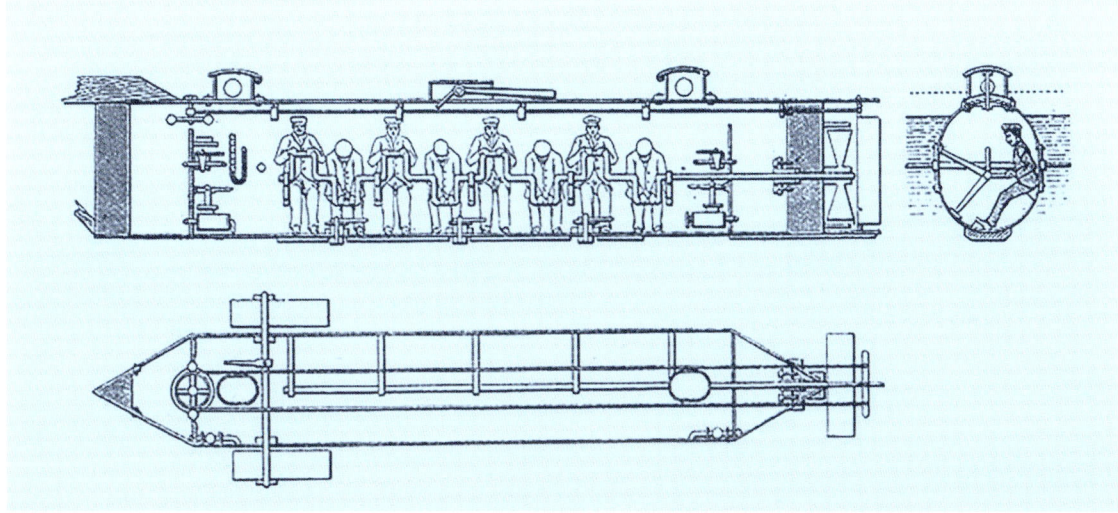

the *Hunley* arrived in Charleston Harbor, Southern military officials seized it and turned it over to the Confederate army. By order of Southern General P. G. T. Beauregard, from then on the *Hunley* would serve as a Confederate army vessel, although Horace Hunley and his partners would continue to be involved in its testing and operations.

Two incidents followed that seemed to spell the end for the *Hunley*. Once the South took control of the submarine, Confederate navy lieutenant John Payne volunteered to be its captain. At the same time, sailors from two Confederate warships signed up to serve as her crew. On August 29, 1863, while the *Hunley* was moored to a steamship prior to making a test dive, Payne accidentally stepped on the device that controlled the ship's diving mechanism, causing the *Hunley* to dive beneath the surface with her hatches still open. Five crew members died in the sinking. The *Hunley* was salvaged, but two months later another disastrous training accident took place. On October 15, 1863, Horace Hunley himself led another seven-man crew as they planned to demonstrate how the submarine worked by diving under a ship in Charleston Harbor. They dove but failed to return, killing all aboard, including Hunley.

Weeks later the submarine was found and was once again brought to the surface and repaired. Despite its tragic history, in November 1863, Confederate navy lieutenant George Dixon agreed to take command of the vessel and to raise a seven-man volunteer crew. It would be Dixon and this crew (Frank Collins, Joseph Ridgeway, James Wicks, Arnold Becker, J. F. Carlsen, C. Lumpkin, and a man only by his last name, Miller) who would make naval history. On the clear, cold, moonlit night of February 17, 1864, John Crosby, the officer of the deck aboard the Union's mightiest sloop of war, the USS *Housatonic*, stood gazing across the waters of Charleston Harbor. At about 8:45 p.m. he saw something moving

just below the surface only about a hundred yards away on the starboard (right) side. Was it a porpoise? Perhaps it was floating debris. But as the object moved closer to the warship Crosby became truly alarmed. He might be mistaken, he thought, but he was certain that the object moving relentlessly toward the *Housatonic* was a submarine.

Aboard the *Hunley*, Lieutenant Dixon was aware that, given the submarine's history, he had been ordered to stay on the surface during any attacks. But as the *Hunley* moved close to the large Union vessel, it was below the waterline. Slightly submerged, it was now so close to the enemy ship that the *Housatonic*'s twelve cannons were useless. Instead, the *Housatonic*'s crew fired their rifles and shotguns, only to see their bullets bounce harmlessly off the *Hunley*'s iron sides. Suddenly, the torpedo, attached to the long pole at the bow of the *Hunley*, slammed into the side of the *Housatonic*, near its powder magazine. As the "torpedo's" 135

The USS *Housatonic* was an important vessel in the North's attempt to blockade key Southern ports.

pounds of gunpowder exploded, the Union ship took on water and within minutes dropped to the bottom of the harbor. The USS *Housatonic* had become the first warship in history to have been sunk by a submarine.

Most of the *Housatonic*'s 155 crewmembers saved themselves by launching lifeboats or by climbing into the ship's rigging, which towered safely above the harbor's shallow twenty-seven-foot depth. Five Union sailors, however, died in the sinking. Meantime, what of the *Hunley*? After slamming her "torpedo" into the side of the *Housatonic*, she reversed herself and had seemingly set course for her home base on Sullivan's Island at the entrance to Charleston Harbor. Later, there were reports that she had shown a blue light, a prearranged signal that indicated she had safely completed her mission. But she was never seen again. For more than the next one hundred years, the fate of the *Hunley* presented archaeologists, scholars, and the public in general with one of their greatest mysteries. What happened to the vessel and her crew?

In 1995, the world got an answer to this question, and it came from a unique source. Novelist Clive Cussler was one of the most successful of all authors. His undersea adventures sold tens of millions of copies. In Cussler's books, the various heroes work for a fictitious agency called the National Underwater and Marine Agency. In real life, Cussler turned fiction into fact by using his wealth to create a real-life National Underwater and Marine Agency (NUMA), which is "dedicated to preserving our maritime heritage through the discovery, archaeological survey, and conservation of shipwreck artifacts." Since its establishment, NUMA has been responsible for the discovery of scores of shipwrecks. And in May 1995, a NUMA search expedition, led by Clive Cussler, found the *Hunley*.

CLIVE CUSSLER

He was a true renaissance man—a best-selling author, an undersea adventurer, and a discoverer of long-lost ships. When he died in 2020, newspapers around the world were filled with tributes to the man who was most responsible for the discovery of the sunken *H. L. Hunley*. One of the most personal of these tributes came from journalist Kellen Butler. "Clive [Cussler]," Butler wrote, "was the heart and soul of this project [to find the *Hunley*]. His commitment to maritime history was contagious and he had a deep love for the team he worked with to find the *Hunley*."

Clive Cussler was born in Aurora, Illinois, in 1931 and grew up in California. After serving in the air force during the Korean War, he entered the field of advertising, where he won many awards for the radio and television ads he created. In the mid-1960s, he turned his attention to writing books and achieved tremendous success with his creation of one of the most beloved characters in modern adventure fiction. His name was Dirk Pitt, and in more than twenty-five best-selling books, Cussler kept readers wondering how Pitt

would ever get out of his latest seemingly impossible situation.

In 1979, Cussler brought the exciting fictitious world he had created to life when he founded the National Underwater and Marine Agency (NUMA), the same organization dedicated to searching for some of history's most famous shipwrecks that helped make his novels so popular. However, it was Clive Cussler, not Dirk Pitt, who made the recovery of long-lost treasures like the *H. L. Hunley* possible.

Cussler articulated a simple explanation of what motivated him. "I have never made claim to being an archaeologist," he stated. "I'm purely an [adventurer] who loves the challenge of solving a mystery; and there is no greater mystery than a lost shipwreck."

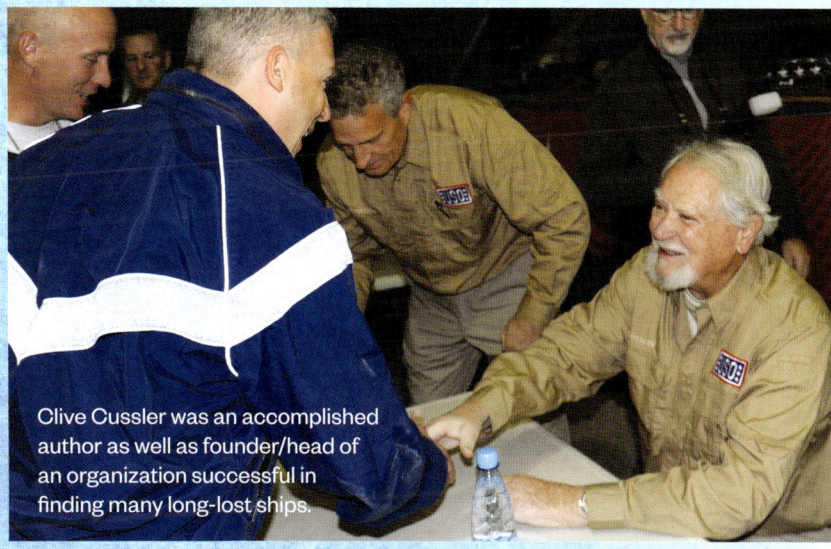

Clive Cussler was an accomplished author as well as founder/head of an organization successful in finding many long-lost ships.

The sunken submarine was discovered lying one hundred yards away and on the seaward side of the *Housatonic*. With the help of a magnetometer and side-scan sonar, the crew identified a large metal object about four miles off the coast of Sullivan's Island, located in Charleston Harbor. They dove thirty feet and then removed another three feet of sediment before uncovering one of the *Hunley*'s two small conning towers. The discovery of the vessel that had forever changed the nature of naval warfare caused a worldwide sensation.

But the big question still remained. What had happened to the *Hunley* and to its crew? After many dives and examinations, it was determined that the layers of silt that had covered the submarine for so long had preserved it well enough that it could be brought to the surface intact. For many months a large team of experts from such organizations as the Naval Historical Center's Underwater Archaeology Branch, the National Park Service, and the South Carolina Institute of Archaeology and Anthropology, along with many talented individuals, examined the sunken *Hunley*, measured her, and documented every facet of her physical makeup. Once they completed their work, it was time to raise the now historic vessel.

First, workmen, specifically hired for the purpose, placed strong harnesses under the submarine and then attached them to a huge crane that sat upon a recovery barge. Then, ever so slowly and carefully, the world's first successful combat submarine was lifted out of the silt and clay of the harbor bottom. On August 8, 2000, in a scene reminiscent of what had taken place when the *Mary Rose* had been raised, church bells rang, cannons boomed, and vessels large and small sounded their horns and rang their bells. An enormous crowd, which included a beaming Cussler, cheered from the shore as, for the first time in more than 136 years, the *Hunley* broke the surface. The sub was taken directly to the Warren Lasch Conservation Center in Charleston and put into a specially designed 75,000 gallon freshwater conservation tank.

Ever since the *Hunley* was placed in this tank, researchers and scientists have been painstakingly cleaning a century-and-a-half of sand, sediment, corrosion, and encrustation from the world's first successful combat submarine. It is difficult, even hazardous work, requiring special suits and involving chemicals

Preserving the *Hunley*, shown here in its conservation tank, was as vital as finding the vessel.

with high pH levels. But the prospect of solving the mystery of what happened to the *Hunley* and its crew drives the restorers on. "It's like unwrapping a Christmas gift after [many] years," says Paul Mardikian, senior conservator of the *Hunley* restoration. "We have been wanting to do this for many years now."

The restoration yielded some of the *Hunley*'s long-held secrets. Archaeologists and scientists, for example, had never been quite sure exactly how the submarine was propelled. The relentless cleaning of the vessel uncovered, hidden beneath the layers of

THE *TURTLE*

The *Hunley* was the first submarine to sink an enemy ship, but it was not the first sub to be used in wartime, nor was it the first to attack an enemy vessel. That distinction belongs to an American Revolutionary War submersible craft named the *Turtle* (also called *American Turtle*).

The *Turtle* was built by David Bushnell, an American inventor. While a student at Yale University, he began building underwater mines. Convinced that the best way to deliver his mines during wartime would be by submarine, he constructed a hand-powered, wooden, underwater vessel large enough to accommodate one operator. He named it *Turtle* because he thought it looked like two turtle shells stuck to one another. It actually looked more like a large clam.

The primitive submarine, which held enough air for about a thirty-minute submersion, was about seven feet long and about six feet tall. It was propelled vertically and horizontally by hand-cranked propellers, dove by allowing water into a tank at its bottom, and rose by allowing water to be pushed out through a hand pump. The only light inside the vessel was provided by a piece of fungus-covered rotting wood, which gave off a soft glow known as foxfire.

When the War of Independence erupted in 1775, Bushnell donated the *Turtle* to the Colonial forces. On September 7, 1776, it made its historic, first-ever attack on an enemy warship when it attempted to sink British Admiral Richard Howe's flagship H.M.S. *Eagle*, which was moored in New York Harbor. A Colonial soldier named Ezra Lee was chosen to operate the sub and carry out the attack, which called for him to stealthily make his way up to the Eagle and attach a time bomb to its hull.

It will never be known why Lee failed to

concretion, a water tube that ran the length of the forty-foot sub. Restorers also discovered a sophisticated set of gears on the crank in the tube that enabled the crew rotating the crank to propel the sub faster by moving water rapidly through the tube. For conservator Johanna Rivera-Diaz, a surprising discovery has been the evidence that one of the crewmen wrapped metal casings around the section of the crank they were responsible for turning and covered them with cloth to prevent blisters from forming on their hands.

One of the most interesting artifacts that has been brought to

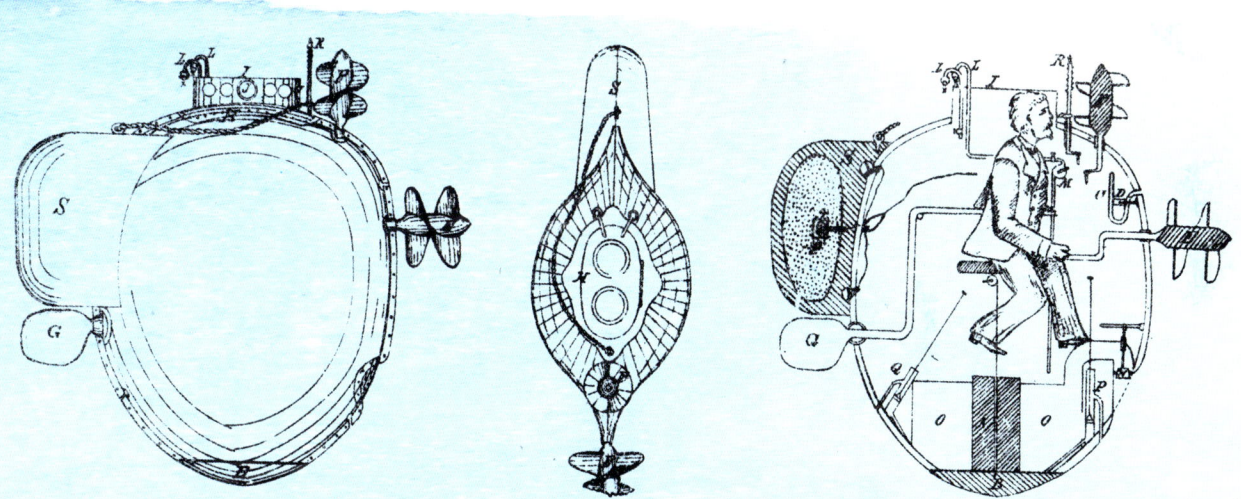

attach the bomb. Some believe it was because he was unable to bore through the *Eagle*'s hull. Perhaps the currents in the harbor were so strong that he could not keep the *Turtle* in the right position long enough to secure the explosive. Whatever the cause, Lee retreated and the bomb exploded nearby without causing damage to either the *Eagle* or the *Turtle*.

During the next week the *Turtle* made several more attempts to sink British ships, but none were successful. Two months later, it met an inglorious end when, during the Battle of Fort Lee, the American ship that was transporting it was sunk by the British. What was not lost, however, was the *Turtle*'s place in history as the first submarine ever to attack an enemy warship.

the surface is a misshapen $20 gold coin, minted in 1860, with the inscription "*Shiloh, April 6th, 1862, My Life Preserver, G. E. D.*" The initials are those of *Hunley* commander George Dixon, who led the attack on the *Housatonic*. Family legend has it that the coin was given to Dixon by a sweetheart to serve as a good luck charm through the Civil War battles. Research has uncovered no such sweetheart. But what is well documented is the fact that Dixon had the coin with him at the Battle of Shiloh, that during the battle a bullet struck him on his thigh, and that the coin in his pocket deflected the bullet, saving his leg and possibly his life.

All of these are interesting revelations, but still the great question remains. Why did the *Hunley* and its eight-man crew never return? A century-and-a-half after it sunk the *Housatonic* and more than twenty years after the submarine was raised, it remains a mystery. But it is one that scientists may be getting closer to solving. Archaeologists, historians, scientists, and other scholars have never lacked speculations as to why the *Hunley* met its fate. One of the most common has been the belief that because the sub was less than twenty feet from the *Housatonic* when the warship exploded, the *Hunley*'s crew was knocked unconscious by the blast and remained so for so long that the air in the vessel ran out before they could awaken. Another popular belief among scientists has been the notion that the crew may have chosen to stay beneath the surface until the ships that came to the *Housatonic*'s aid left the scene. If that was the case, and if they miscalculated and stayed down too long, they would have run out of oxygen and perished.

Other experts have put forth the theory that the *Hunley* may have been hit in a vital spot by a shot from the *Housatonic*. Still others have speculated that the sub was sucked into the vortex of the sinking warship and dragged to the bottom. Adding to the giant mystery is the fact that not only were the remains of the crew found inside the sub, they were found at their positions at the crank. There was no evidence that any of them had made any attempt to flee the vessel. Dr. Rachel Lance

As with all the objects retrieved from the *Hunley*, conservators measured and recorded every detail of the recovered wallet (top).

A wallet found aboard the sunken Hunley (bottom)

This pocket watch was among the crew's personal items discovered during the *Hunley*'s excavation.

leads a team of Duke University researchers seeking answers to the riddle of the *Hunley*. "All the physical evidence points to the crew taking absolutely no action in response to a flood or loss of air," she states.

In what has garnered a great deal of publicity, Lance and her fellow Duke researchers have come up with what they are convinced is the most plausible explanation of what happened to the crew of the *Hunley*. After conducting three years of experiments on a mini test-sub, they believe that the torpedo blast that rocked the *Housatonic* would have created a shock wave through the *Hunley* great enough to rupture the blood vessels in the lungs and brains of those in the submarine. "'This is the characteristic trauma of blast victims, they call it 'blast lung,'" states Dr. Lance. "You have an instant fatality that leaves no marks on the skeletal remains. Unfortunately, the soft tissues that would show us what happened have decomposed in the past hundred years."

The "blast lung" theory has been embraced by a significant number of experts. Other scientists have not been as willing to accept it. Perhaps we will never know the cause for the demise of the submarine and its crew.

CHAPTER SEVEN

THE EREBUS AND THE TERROR

In the early and mid-1800s, England, the most powerful country in the world, had a national obsession. Its government was possessed with the desire to find what English geographic experts were certain was a Northwest Passage through the Arctic. Finding the Passage, they knew, would save hundreds of millions of pounds and countless lives by enabling British merchants to trade directly with East Asia, with its coveted spices and other riches, rather than taking the long, dangerous water route around Asia.

Great Britain's desire to find what became known as the "Arctic Grail," became so intense that between 1818 and 1850 dozens of Passage-seeking expeditions were sent into the frozen North. By 1850, a legion of British naval explorers, including Edward Parry, John Ross, James Clark Ross, and John Franklin, had made what was thought to be so much progress that the nation's leaders

Before taking John Franklin and his crew on their search for the Northwest Passage, the *Erebus* and the *Terror* had a long history of sailing the dangerous but often majestic Arctic seas (opposite page).

James Clark Ross was one of scores of high-ranking British naval officers who devoted much of their lives to finding the Northwest Passage (bottom).

and much of the public were certain that Great Britain was on the doorstep of finding the fabled Passage. What it would take, they believed, was one more determined expedition.

On May 19, 1845, England launched what it thought was that expedition. It was commanded by Sir John Franklin, who had already proved himself on two previous Passage searches. Many people believed that this was indeed the expedition that would bring home the prize, and Franklin and his men were sent into the Arctic aboard two extraordinary ships. They were named the *Erebus* and the *Terror*, and they were the two most celebrated ships in all of Great Britain. Two years earlier the ships had returned to England after successfully transporting explorer James Clark Ross and his men to and from the Antarctic. The *Terror* was particularly famous. It had first come to national attention in 1836 when, despite being battered about by ice floes for almost a year, it had enabled explorer George Back to complete one of the most harrowing of all Arctic searches for the Northwest Passage. The *Terror* was also one of the ships that, during the War of 1812, fired shots on the United States' Fort McHenry, which had led to the song that the Americans now regarded as their national anthem.

Built to bombard enemy shore batteries, the *Erebus* and the *Terror* were known as bomb ships. Made of English oak, they were designed to be strong enough to withstand the weight and recoil of heavy guns and thousands of pounds of shells and explosives. *Erebus* was 105 feet long and weighed 372 tons. The 102-foot long *Terror* weighed 325 tons.

Most important of all, the *Erebus* and the *Terror* were the most technologically advanced ships that had ever entered the Arctic. Unlike any other ships, both vessels were fitted with an internal heating system to protect against the life-threatening Arctic cold. Huge pipes carried steam created in enormous belowdecks boilers, which supplied heat to the officers' cabins and the crew's living quarters. To further protect against subzero temperatures, both ships had double doors attached to all hatches and ladderways.

The most dramatic technological features, however, lay in the way both ships were powered and propelled. In order for the *Erebus* to make its way through the thickest ice fields, the British Admiralty equipped the vessel with a fifteen-ton, twenty-five horsepower railroad locomotive engine. The *Terror* was powered by a similar but slightly smaller engine. At a time when almost all steam vessels were propelled by paddle wheels, which were vulnerable to ice and storms, the *Erebus* and the *Terror* were equipped with screw propellers, which were far more capable of dealing with extreme conditions. The propellers were also designed in such a way that, like the ships' rudders, they were retractable and could be lifted out of harm's way if it appeared that they were about to be destroyed by ice.

Because the Admiralty was determined it would be Franklin's expedition that would at last find the Passage, it also made sure the *Erebus* and the *Terror* were the two best-provisioned ships that had ever entered the Arctic. Each vessel carried enough food and supplies for at least a three-year search. The supplies included almost seventy tons of flour, 3,900 gallons of alcohol, and about three-and-a-half tons of tobacco.

Just as the technological features of the two ships were revolutionary, so too was the nature of the food supplies. The

Erebus and the *Terror* were the first ships to take advantage of a dramatic new invention—the tin can. Aboard the vessels were over eight thousand cans containing a variety of meats, canned vegetables, and different kinds of canned soups.

And there was something else revolutionary about the two ships. No one had any doubt that, like almost all the ships that had gone looking for the Passage, Franklin's vessels would be forced to spend one, two, or even three full winters locked in the ice until a hoped-for spring thaw took place and the search could be resumed. It was a situation that led to one of the greatest challenges of long-term Arctic searching—boredom. In order to keep Franklin's officers and men from succumbing to boredom during their long winter months in the ice, the *Erebus* and the *Terror* each had libraries containing some three thousand books. The two ships also carried theatrical scripts, scores of costumes, and huge quantities of makeup so that plays could be staged for the crew's enjoyment. In addition, both the *Erebus* and the *Terror* had a large printing press, which enabled the publication of a daily ship's newspaper whose purpose was to keep the crew busy with its production and to serve as a source of information and entertainment at a time when very little else was taking place on board.

On May 19, 1845, more than ten thousand cheering people gathered at the docks outside London to see the Franklin expedition off. Given Franklin's reputation as an explorer and the nature of his two ships, many expected this would be the Passage-search that would achieve the long-awaited glorious result. Roderick Murchison, the president of the Royal Geographical Society, seemed to speak for all Great Britain when he proclaimed, "There appears to be but one wish among the whole of the inhabitants of this country, that the enterprise in which the officers and crew are about to be engaged may be attended with success." As the *Erebus* and the *Terror* pulled away from the dock and the cheering grew even louder, one observer became overwhelmed by what was taking place before him. "One would fancy," he exclaimed, "England celebrating Franklin's return rather than his departure."

It was a glorious departure indeed. But there would be no return. In what would become one of the greatest and most-publicized mysteries of all time, John Franklin, his men, and his two extraordinary ships would never be heard from again. Communication with the ships in the Arctic took months at best, and at first, the lack of word either from or about Franklin and his men did not set off national alarm. It was still fully expected that any day Franklin would return in triumph. But by the end of 1847, when still nothing had been heard, public concern began to grow. Where was he? Where were the two greatest ships on the planet? As *Dollar Magazine* proclaimed, "Expectation darkened into anxiety—anxiety into dread."

Something clearly had to be done, and eventually, in the largest search and rescue undertaken in history, dozens of expeditions were sent out in search of the missing explorer and his crew. Those who headed these rescue attempts included almost all of England's leading navigators and explorers. Lady Jane Franklin, Franklin's wealthy and determined wife, instigated and even financed several of the searches. She also persuaded the American president Zachary Taylor to send out two ships with rescuers including Elisha Kent Kane, destined to become one of the world's most famous Arctic adventurers.

Year after year, the searches went on. Graves and skeletons of members of the *Erebus* and the *Terror* were found. Belongings of both officers and the crew were discovered. In 1859, a message found by a search party on King William Island stated that both the *Erebus* and the *Terror* were trapped in ice in late 1846 and remained so for about eighteen months. It added that Franklin had died and that in April 1848, 105 survivors had headed out in search of help. Amazingly, it was the only written message from anyone on the *Erebus* or the *Terror* ever discovered.

By 1860, all British government sponsored searches for Franklin, his men, the *Erebus*, and the *Terror* had come to an end. Sad as it was, most of the public agreed with the decision. The costs of the searches had been staggering, with the English government spending more than fifty million dollars in today's money. At least a dozen ships had been lost in the rescue efforts.

The whereabouts of Franklin and his men would become one of the world's greatest mysteries, inspiring scores of books, poems, and ballads. And the *Erebus* and the *Terror* would become the most sought-after prizes in marine archaeology— a Holy Grail. Then, in 2008, the Canadian government's archaeological organization Parks Canada began to search for the two fabled ships.

From the beginning, there was a huge difference in the way Parks Canada conducted its search from all the previous hunts for the two fabled ships: finally, they prioritized seeking information using oral histories. Beginning with the earliest seekers of the

American explorer Elisha Kent Kane was one of countless individuals who risked their lives in the search for the Northwest Passage, the search for John Franklin, or both.

SIDE-SCAN SONAR

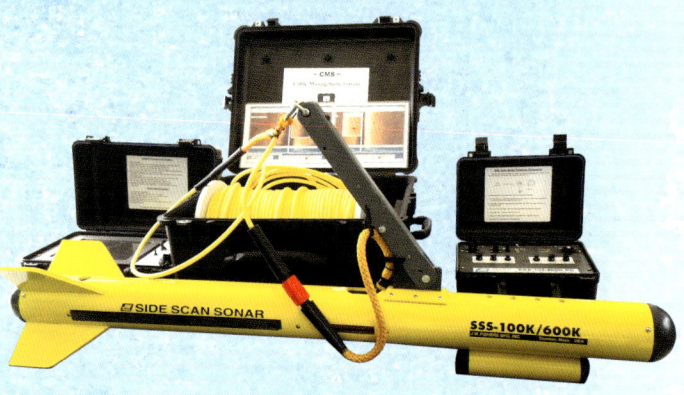

Of all the innovations and technical advancements that have made the discovery and excavation of shipwrecks increasingly possible, none has been more important than the invention and continual development of side-scan sonar.

The term sonar is short for "sound navigation and ranging." It is a tool that allows scientists to use sound waves to explore the ocean. Since its invention, one of the most important uses of sonar, particularly the underwater ocean tool known as side-scan sonar, is its use in locating sunken ships and artifacts that lie within and around them. Marine archaeologists also use side-scan sonar for developing nautical charts, locating underwater hazards, and mapping the seafloor.

Side-scan sonar is a type of sonar system that can be towed through the water from a surface vessel or a submarine, or mounted on a ship's hull. As the ship or submarine moves along, the transducer array within the side-scan sonar sends out signals on both of its sides, sweeping the ocean floor like a fan-shaped flashlight beam, sending data to a computer aboard the surface vessel. The "pictures" that emerge are made up of dark and light areas. For example, detected hard objects send up both a strong echo and a dark image. Soft areas and shadows such as sand and mud send up weaker echoes and lighter images.

Side-scan sonar has been widely used to detect obstructions on the ocean floor that might be hazardous to shipping or to seabed installations by the gas and oil industries. It has been deployed also by the military for mine detection, to search for lost submarines and, in one highly publicized case, to search for a hydrogen bomb lost at sea.

For historians, anthropologists, and marine archaeologists, the most important use of side-scan sonar is in the location and excavation of shipwrecks. One of the very first practical uses of side-scan sonar took place in 1963 when a team made up of Edward Curley, John Yules, and the brilliant inventor Dr. Harold Edgerton used an early version of side-scan sonar to find the sunken *Vineyard Lightship* in Buzzards Bay, Massachusetts. From 1963 to 1966, significant improvements on this early system were made by scientist Martin Klein, generally considered to be the "father" of commercial side-scan sonar.

It was in 1967 that Dr. Edgerton used side-scan sonar to help Andrew McKee find the long-sought-for *Mary Rose*. It was also in 1967 that side-scan sonar proved indispensable in helping George Bass find what was then the world's oldest shipwreck off the coast of Uluburun, Turkey.

Northwest Passage, most who sought that Holy Grail had never bothered to ask any of the region's Inuit residents if they knew anything about two ships that resembled the *Erebus*, the *Terror*, or about more than 120 white men who appeared to be in desperate straits. But the Inuit did know, and among their descendants was a highly respected Inuit elder and schoolteacher named Louie Kamookak. Before Kamookak died in 2018, he had spent the last forty years trying to solve the Franklin mystery.

For generations, the Inuit did not have a written language. But they have a rich oral history filled with stories about their

Every British expedition that sailed to the Arctic had an artist aboard who produced dramatic, detailed depiction of the searchers' experiences.

past that continues to this day. From an early age, Kamookak had been fascinated with these tales, particularly those that had to do with John Franklin and his ill-fated expedition. "I first started hearing [Franklin] stories as far as I start remembering," he said, "maybe age six or seven. When I started going to school . . . that's when the teacher started talking about the Franklin expedition. How it happened on King William Island. How all of them died. They didn't get back. The ships were never found."

As Kamookak grew up listening to elders' stories about Franklin and his men and it became an obsession. "If it was a Franklin story," he stated, "I was always there to listen." The more stories he heard, the more he became convinced that if the *Erebus* and the *Terror* were to be discovered they would be found on King William Island, the very island upon which he had spent most of his life. "Louie," states John Geiger, "was someone who devoted [more than] three decades of his life to understanding the puzzles and the clues surrounding the disappearance of the two ships."

For Kamookak, a vital part of that search was comparing Inuit stories with the logbooks and journals written by the many explorers who had gone looking for Franklin. Inuit histories reported people finding dismembered bodies and fragments of china on King William Island. His own great-grandmother's story of discovering a grave there indicating a body buried underground—not wrapped in fur and sent out to sea in the Inuit style–particularly stuck with Kamookak. And other Inuit stories dating back to the time of the ships' disappearance reported that some even claimed to have boarded a vessel in the area and seen a grinning corpse sitting upright in the captain's cabin.

By the 1980s, he had become known among the other Franklin searchers as an indispensable source of information. Throughout the 1980s and 1990s, he accompanied David Woodman and other searchers on their treks. By 2014, Kamookak had convinced a team of Franklin seekers from Parks Canada to follow his guidance to King William Island. And after all the long and frustrating years of searching, the Erebus was discovered in shallow water, in near perfect condition.

Two years later, as the Parks Canada team continued its search for the second missing vessel, another Inuit person would play a key role in a second great discovery.

On September 2, 2016, the Parks Canada team was headed in one direction when a new crew member, an Inuit man named Sammy Kogvik, startled his companions by telling them how, while on a fishing trip, he had spotted a tall piece of wood sticking out of the ice at Terror Bay, just south of King William Island. That was six years prior, and after he took a photo of the piece of wood but lost the film, he had mostly forgotten all about it. But now that he was on a mission so focused on finding such a long-sought-after prize, he realized that the tall piece of wood could well have been a mast. Could it have been part of the *Terror*?

Immediately after hearing Kogvik's story, search leaders ordered the ship to head, directly to Terror Bay. There, on September 2, 2016, in relatively shallow water, the H.M.S. *Terror* was found. The discovery of the ship at a spot almost precisely predicted by Kamookak was, to many, truly astounding. What was equally amazing was the condition of the wreck. Thanks to the frigid Arctic waters, the *Terror*'s state of preservation shocked its Parks

A sonar image of the HMS *Erebus* shows where it came to rest on the seafloor, remarkably intact.

The almost two-hundred-yearlong search for the men of the Franklin expedition was the most adventurous, harrowing, and closely followed maritime search in history.

HMS *INVESTIGATOR*

Remarkably, the *Erebus* and the *Terror* are not the only long-lost ships connected with the Franklin saga to be discovered. In July 2010, members of a special Parks Canada expedition found the HMS *Investigator*, the ship that found the Northwest Passage before becoming trapped in the ice for more than two years.

It is an extraordinary story, a tale of what began as a rescue mission requiring a rescue of its own. It began on January 20, 1850, when the HMS *Investigator*, captained by Robert McClure, and the HMS *Enterprise*, captained by Richard Collinson, left England in search of John Franklin and his men. The two ships were supposed to travel together but McClure, obsessed with finding the Northwest Passage first and not the most honest of men, managed to slip away from Collinson, arrived in the Arctic first, and in a voyage in which he continually put his ship and his men recklessly at risk, actually found the coveted Passage. Attempting to return home, however, he managed to become trapped in Mercy Bay, where he and his sixty men remained for almost three years.

In April 1853, with many of them in desperate physical condition, the crew of the HMS *Investigator* was rescued by a sledge party from the HMS *Resolute*, another British vessel searching for the Franklin party.

Eventually, they were brought back to England, where McClure and his men received cash rewards for their historic achievement. Meantime, the abandoned *Investigator* sank beneath the ice.

In 2010, Parks Canada discovered the *Investigator* more rapidly than anyone could have anticipated. Based on old charts and journals, Parks Canada searchers had a general idea of where they believed the sunken ship originally lay. But they had no idea how far it may have drifted over so many years. They had, in fact, arrived prepared to search for sixteen hours a day for two weeks. But three minutes after they began a sonar scan at the spot where they thought the vessel might be, they found it.

The discovery of the Northwest Passage after centuries of searches was truly a historic achievement. But despite the attention Robert McClure, his men, and their ship received, they never got the acclaim they would have if their nation's attention had not been so completely focused on the various searches for Franklin. Parks Canada's archeologist Ryan Harris hopes that the discovery of the ship will change that. "Our goal," he says, "is to remove *Investigator* from the margins of history."

Canada discoverers. "The wreck," states archaeologist Adrian Schimnowski, "is in such good condition that glass panes are still in three of four tall windows in the stern cabin where the ship's commander, Captain Francis Crozier, slept and worked. This vessel looks like it was buttoned down tight for winter and it sank. . . . If you could lift this boat out of the water and pump the water out, it would probably float."

Given the extreme weather conditions that constantly plague the area around where both the *Erebus* and the *Terror* lie, excavating the wrecks present an enormous challenge. The weather in this section of the Arctic in particular is, in fact, so harsh that exploration and excavation around the sites have been possible for just a few weeks each year in August and September. It is a frustrating obstacle since perhaps the most incredible aspect about the entire Franklin affair is that, aside from the one note discovered in 1859, not a single piece of written evidence from an expedition led by a man known for his detailed record keeping has ever been found.

In the face of these huge challenges, Parks Canada's marine archaeologists and researchers are utilizing the latest state-of-the-art, cutting-edge tools and technology to solve the mysteries of the Franklin expedition in general, and the *Erebus* and the *Terror* in particular. As Sam Macdonald, the president of the underwater robotics company Deep Trekker, has stated, "The technologies available now, even compared to five or six years ago, are incredible."

Among the most innovative of these new tools is a small underwater robot also officially named Deep Trekker but given the name "Neptune" in honor of the dog that accompanied the Franklin expedition. About the size of a basketball, Neptune, according to those who have seen it in action, "can get into some really tight places." In the limited amount of time that the harsh weather has allowed it to explore the *Erebus*, Neptune has provided from inside the crushed remains of John Franklin's cabin. "Only the Deep Trekker could shimmy in there," says Ryan Harris.

Neptune promises to be an important discovery and excavation tool not only for those involved in the recovery of the *Erebus* and the *Terror* but for all those involved in future shipwreck excavations—as does another recent technological advancement being utilized by Parks Canada. It is called multibeam echo sounder technology and it can provide a 3-D topographical map of the ocean floor and any structures, including shipwrecks, that are lying there. Parks Canada is also taking advantage of another technological development called stereophotogrammetry, which produces pictures in pairs and then synthesizes hundreds of these pairings to produce extraordinarily clear images of whatever object is being studied. "We used this to form a 3-D base map of the *Erebus* wreck site, which amounts to millions and millions and millions of 3-D data points that are accurate within a few millimeters, so it allows a structural snapshot of what the wreck was like at a particular time," states Harris.

These examples of the latest in underwater discovery technology are not the only high-tech tools that will soon be available to all those seeking the evidence of the past from shipwrecks. Surface vessels are now developed with, among other advanced features, multibeam sonar built into the bottom of the ship and have the ability to feed video from deep under the sea directly to a website, where interested parties can watch.

Given the enormous obstacles from the harshest weather on earth the excavators of the *Erebus* and the *Terror* face, unlocking the secrets of the two long-lost ships is taking more time than those involved in the project would prefer. But, in the spirit of all those who have devoted much of their lives to recovering the past from the ocean floor, they will persevere and prove once again that, as far as marine archaeology is concerned, it is not what we find, but what we find out.

The search for sunken vessels, often carried out in the most daunting of circumstances, has, throughout history, been one of the most challenging of all adventures.

FOR FURTHER EXPLORATION

While the number of ships that lie sunken on the ocean floor is truly amazing, so too is the number of shipwrecks that have been discovered and, in many cases, excavated. Here are a few that you might want to explore further.

THE WORLD'S OLDEST INTACT SHIPWRECK

"It's like another world," declares the Black Sea Maritime Archaeology Project (MAP)'s Helen Farr. "It's when the ROV [remote operated vehicle] drops down through the water column, and you see this ship appear in the light at the bottom so perfectly preserved, it feels like you step back in time." The ship that she's talking about is a vessel that her project discovered more than a mile below the surface in the Black Sea, off the coast of Bulgaria. Experts have determined that it is the world's oldest shipwreck, and that the vessel has lain undisturbed at the bottom of the sea for more than 2,400 years. "A ship surviving intact from the classical world, lying in over [a mile] of water, is something I would never have thought possible," states Professor Jon Adams, MAP's principal investigator who played a key role in finding the ancient ship in October 2018. "This will change our understanding of shipbuilding and seafaring in the ancient world."

THE AMAZING GLASS WRECK

In 1973, a Turkish official made an exploratory dive to check out a report that sponge divers had brought handfuls of brilliantly colored glass from the bottom of a bay called Serçe Limani. The official resurfaced from his dive exclaiming, "There is glass everywhere." In 1977, the Institute of Nautical Archaeology (INA), led by George Bass, launched an excavation of the Serçe Limani site. The brilliantly colored glass was cargo being carried by a two-masted Byzantine merchant ship around the year 1025. The amount of glass in various shapes, sizes, and colors was truly staggering—as many as twenty thousand pieces.

Glass objects from the Byzantine era were extremely rare. What if the glass fragments could be pieced together into the original cups, vases, dishes, and other glassware? To solve what amounted to one of history's greatest jigsaw puzzles, the INA put together a team of Turkish and American archaeology students and put them to work. Eventually, the student sorters were joined by six local glass menders, a professional glass conservator, and two illustrators. The glass mending went on nonstop, twelve months a year, for twenty years. "We saw," stated Bass, "the local glass menders, who joined us right out of school, not only become experts, but marry and raise children." When they finished they had performed a miracle. They had restored thousands of bowls, bottles, vases, cups, jars, jugs, beakers, and plates in more than two hundred different shapes. No one understood the magnitude of the accomplishment more than George Bass. What has been assembled, he proclaimed, "is by far the greatest collection of Islamic glass in the world."

YASSI ADA

In 1958, Kemal Aras, the Turkish sponge diver who had discovered the shipwreck at Cape Gelidonya and had taken Peter Throckmorton to see it, took Throckmorton to the site of another shipwreck he had discovered. This one was off the coast of a small island called Yassi Ada, which lay off the coast of Turkey. After diving down to the sunken vessel, Throckmorton returned to the surface boat almost as excited as he had been after first investigating the Gelidonya wreck. "This," he would later state, "was a shipwreck of a period never before investigated, the time of the beginning of the Byzantine Empire."

As soon as he could, Throckmorton informed George Bass of the find. When the excavations at Cape Gelidonya were completed, he and his team headed for Yassi Ada. There they were joined by archaeologists and divers from the newly formed Institute of Nautical Archaeology (INA). Also joining the group, and destined to play a key role in the excavations that followed, was Frederick van Doorninck, Jr., one of Bass's fellow doctoral students from the University of Pennsylvania.

The recovery operations at Yassi Ada were carried out from 1961 to 1964 and required 3,533 dives. One of the first things that divers discovered was that the sunken ship was constructed in such a way that, unlike almost all wooden ships built before it, the strength of this hull came not from its planking but from its internal framing system. This innovation places the vessel at an important transitional stage in ship-building technology.

The most striking discovery of all was that the ship was carrying almost one thousand amphorae (huge ancient jugs), most of which contained wine. Many of the amphorae were covered with written notations, which indicated previous uses such as storing olives or lentils. During the 1961–1964 excavations, 110 of the amphorae were brought to the surface. Because the notations on so many of them had the potential of providing important clues as to where the ship originated and exactly what route it took before it met its fate, during a 1980 revisit to Yassi Ada, 570 additional amphorae were found and brought to the surface.

LA TRINITÉ

As archaeologist Chuck Meide has written, "In the world of ships and treasures there's really no better story than *La Trinité*. It is critical to the origin story of . . . America. It's also the first example of a group that faced religious persecution in Europe coming to America to seek freedom." The story begins in 1565 when a fleet of seven French ships, led by Captain Jean Ribault, sailed out of France and headed for the French settlement of Fort Caroline on the northeast coast of Florida. The ships were loaded with guns and other munitions, gold, silver, foodstuffs, livestock, and nearly a thousand sailors and Protestant colonists called Huguenots seeking freedom in the New World. The goals of the venture were to restock the settlement at Fort Caroline and, equally important, to enable France to establish a foothold in America, much of which had already been claimed by France's archrival Spain.

The majority of the French ships made it to Fort Caroline, but on the way, disaster struck when Ribault's flagship, *La Trinité*, and three other vessels were caught in a vicious storm and sank. For more than 450 years *La Trinité*, filled not only with immense treasure but also artifacts of a New World settlement fifty-five years before the Pilgrims, was the continual object of intense search. Then, in May 2016, veteran underseas treasure hunter Bobby Pritchett found it off the coast of Cape Canaveral, Florida. Like the treasure ship the *San José*, *La Trinité* has been the subject of intense debate and legal proceedings between various parties—in this case Pritchett, Florida, and France—over who owns the rights to the enormously valuable shipwreck. Pritchett has backed his claim by pointing out that his long search for the vessel was carried out in the most scientific manner possible. Archaeologist James Delgado has backed the case for his fellow scientists by stating, "We don't want artifacts ending up on a mantelpiece or in a private collection instead of taking us on a journey of understanding."

SANTO ANTONIO DE TANNA

In the long history of nations and seafaring, there has rarely been a country more powerful on the sea than was Portugal in the 1500s. The discovery, albeit accidental, of a whole New World in 1492 and the finding of the long sought-after water trade route to India in 1498 had enabled a relatively poor nation of only 1.3 million people to build an empire that extended from Brazil to China. It was not to last.

By 1697, when the Portuguese ship *Santo Antonio de Tanna* sank off the coast of Africa, the British and the Dutch were successfully challenging Portugal's sea trading monopoly, and the Omani Arabs were rebelling against more than one hundred years of Portuguese oppression. In 1696, this rebellion came to full flower when an Arab force sailed into an African harbor at Mombasa and laid siege to the vital Portuguese fort at Fort Jesus.

On Christmas Day, 1696, a Portuguese relief force in the form of four ships, led by the heavily armed frigate the *Santo Antonio de Tanna*, arrived in the waters directly in front of the fort. In the battle that followed, the *Santo Antonio*, one of the most important ships remaining in the Portuguese fleet, was sunk. And there it remained until 1960 when it was discovered by Kenyan divers Conway Plough and Peter Philips. Between 1976 and 1981, it became the first Portuguese ship ever to be scientifically excavated.

SAN JOSÉ

Its name was the *San José* and it was part of a Spanish fleet that, during the War of the Spanish Succession (1701–1714), was sailing from Portobelo, Panama, to Cartagena, Colombia. On June 8, 1708, the fleet encountered a British squadron and, during the fierce naval battle that followed, the *San José* exploded, sending the ship and almost all of its six-hundred-man crew to the bottom. Also aboard the vessel was an extraordinary amount of gold, silver, emeralds, and other jewels, and more than eleven million coins, all collected in the South American colonies to finance the Spanish king's war effort. Estimates by maritime experts have placed the value of this amazing cargo at about 20 billion dollars.

For centuries, the *San José* lay lost on the ocean floor. Then, on November 27, 2015, it was finally discovered by a remotely operated submarine (ROV) operated by the Woods Hole Oceanographic Institution. Rather than lead to an excavation of the vessel, however, the discovery touched off years of dispute between Spain, for whom the ship sailed, Colombia, in whose waters its shipwreck was found, and an American company, Sea Search Armada, that has claimed that it found the ship years before the ROV made its find. The dispute over who has the rights to what might be the richest ship ever to sail the seas continues today with no signs of a resolution in sight.

USS MONITOR

There is no more famous nor arguably more important American naval vessel than the USS *Monitor*, which in its historic battle with the Confederate ironclad, the CSS *Virginia*, heralded the end of combat at sea between wooden ships. Also notable for its revolutionary revolving turret that, for the first time, allowed a warship to fire in every direction, the *Monitor* sank in turbulent waters off Cape Hatteras, North Carolina, on December 31, 1862, as she headed to join a Union fleet assembling for an attack on the Confederate stronghold of Charleston, South Carolina.

It was hardly surprising that as one of the most historically important vessels in naval history, the *Monitor* would spawn a great many searches. And it did. Yet, for more than 100 years it lay undetected at the bottom of the ocean. Then, in 1973, a team of scientists from Duke University's Maritime Laboratory found the historic ironclad. Since then, vital sections of the *Monitor*, most notably its revolving turret, have been brought to the surface. In 1975, in order to protect it from looters or treasure hunters, the shipwreck site was designated the Monitor National Marine Sanctuary (MNMS), the first of these types of protected areas in the nation. This sanctuary has not only set an important precedent in the protection of shipwrecks but has also led to another significant development.

In examining the sanctuary's large site, a largely unknown or forgotten aspect of World War II has come to light. Based on what divers and researchers have discovered and concluded, from 1942 to 1945, the seas where the *Monitor* went down were an important

World War II battlefield. During that period, in the waters off Cape Hatteras, German submarines sank more than eighty merchant tankers, freighters, and Allied warships, and hundreds of people, most of them merchant marines, were killed. Along with continuing to protect and preserve the remains of the USS *Monitor*, MNMS's expanded mission will be to explore these World War II shipwrecks, and, if possible, to recover relics and educate the public about this maritime battlefield that, while so close to home, has all but been lost to history.

USS INDIANAPOLIS

The USS *Indianapolis* was a highly decorated United States warship that as, the U.S. Navy has stated, "is primarily remembered for her worst 15 minutes." In July 1945, the *Indy*, as she was called, completed one of the most secret missions of World War II. She delivered critical parts of the world's first atomic bomb to the island of Tinian. On July 30, 1945, as she headed home via the Philippine Sea, she was suddenly hit by torpedoes fired by a Japanese submarine. There were nearly 1,200 sailors aboard the ship, and about three hundred of them died as the ship went down. The remaining nine hundred were thrown into the sea, where most of them eventually died from dehydration, starvation, salt poisoning, and shark attacks. Adding to the tragedy was the fact that the U.S. Navy never realized that the *Indianapolis* was overdue at its next port of call and never sent a rescue party to the disaster site.

The sunken ship lay on the ocean floor for more than seventy-two years until, on August 19, 2017, a team headed by Microsoft cofounder Paul Allen discovered it lying some 18,000 feet beneath the sea. Allen, like Clive Cussler, has devoted much of his life to searching for and recovering shipwrecks. Because the wreck lies so deep in the sea, it will probably take years before the equipment is in place to excavate it. Meantime, its discovery has brought closure to many of the families who lost loved ones in the sinking. The U.S. government has awarded a Congressional Gold Medal collectively to the crew of the *Indianapolis*.

THE *ENDURANCE*

On March 9, 2022, an Antarctic search team made a stunning announcement. After being lost in the Antarctic's Weddell Sea since 1915, one of the most physically challenging places in the world, famed polar explorer Ernest Shackleton's equally famous ship, the *Endurance*, was discovered approximately ten thousand feet beneath the ice-packed surface.

"The discovery of the wreck is an incredible achievement," declared the search team's leader Dr. John Sears. "We have successfully completed the world's most difficult shipwreck search, battling constantly shifting sea-ice, blizzards, and temperatures dropping down to –18C. We have achieved what many people said was impossible."

The story of Shackleton's attempt to make the first land crossing of Antarctica, the *Endurance*, which was the expedition's ship, and Shackleton's personal heroic adventures in bringing help to his men once they and their ship were hopelessly trapped, is one of history's greatest adventure sagas. The discovery of the legendary vessel made headlines around the world. Under the terms of the International Antarctic Treaty, the *Endurance* shipwreck is a designated historic monument and must not be disturbed in any way. Thus, as of the date of publication of this book, no physical artifacts from the vessel have been brought to the surface.

SOURCE NOTES

The source of each quotation in this book is found below. The citation indicates the first and last words of the quotation and its document source. The sources are listed either in the bibliography or below.

INTRODUCTION

"Before there were . . . expanses of open water.": Bass, *Beneath the Seven Seas*.

CHAPTER ONE: ANTIKYTHERA

"A heap of . . . green corpses.": Throckmorton, *The Sea Remembers*.

"The ship that . . . floating museum.": Goldbaum, Elizabeth, "Ancient Greek 'Antikythera' Shipwreck Still Holds Secrets," *Live Science*, June 23, 2015.

"It's kind of . . . whole suit.": Baehr, Leslie G., "The Exosuit Comes Aboard," *Oceanus*, September 11, 2014.

"We found bones . . . a skull.": Kaplan, Sarah, "Scientists uncovered a skeleton from the ancient world's most famous—and mysterious—shipwreck," *Washington Post*, September 20, 2016.

"Human remains have . . . these people.": Jayaraj, Nandita, "What a 2,000-Year-Old Skeleton Tells Us About a Mysterious Shipwreck," *The Wire*, September 21, 2016.

"Not only are . . . and perfumes.": Ibid.

"We're down in . . . Tut's tomb.": Sample. Ian, "Antikythera shipwreck yields bronze arm—and hints at spectacular haul of statutes," *Guardian*, October 4, 2017.

"Ancient Bronze sculpture . . . be missed.": Ibid.

"The *Titanic* . . . ancient world.": Woods Hole Oceanographic Institution, "Stunning Finds from Ancient Greek Shipwreck," press release, October 9, 2014.

"Were they sailing . . . the other?": Wei-Haas, Maya, "Antikythera Shipwreck Yields New Cache of Ancient Treasures," *Smithsonian* magazine, September 29, 2015.

"This is the . . . underwater archaeology.": Marchant, Jo, "Divers return to famous Antikythera wreck to hunt for new treasures," *New Scientist*, September 23, 2015.

CHAPTER TWO: CAPE GELIDONYA

"extremely dangerous to mariners.": Pliny the Elder, *The Natural History*, Book IV, translated by Henry T. Riley and John Bostock, 1855.

"If . . . world's richest lottery.": Throckmorton, *The Sea Remembers*.

"I was convinced . . . sea remembered.": Ibid.

"Here I am . . . the director.": Geiger, Dale, "The Underwater World of George Bass," *Johns Hopkins Magazine*, April 1997.

"Could there possible . . . ever found.": Bass, George, "A Bronze Age Shipwreck," *Expedition*, Winter 1961.

"Nothing much could . . . underwater.": Marx, *Treasure Lost at Sea*.

"I had no . . . changing forever.": Geiger, Dale, "The Underwater World of George Bass," *Johns Hopkins Magazine*, April 1997.

"I honestly can't . . . I do.": Keiger, Dale, "The Underwater World of George Bass."

"I always say . . . the library.": Ibid.

"I'm proud that . . . of archaeology.": Ibid.

"No one had . . . three months.": Bass, *Beneath the Seven Seas*.

"A lot of . . . in that.": Bass, quoted in "The Underwater World of George Bass," *Johns Hopkins Magazine*, April 1997.

"was that we . . . tell us.": Throckmorton, *The Sea Remembers*.

"At Cape Gelidonya . . . sea bottom.": Ibid.

"The first job . . . Turkish beach.": Ibid.

"One of the . . . generations before.": Ibid.

"Why does a . . . Canaanite.": Bass, quoted in "The Underwater World of George Bass," *Johns Hopkins Magazine*, April 1997.

"that came before . . . ocean forever.": "Cape Gelidonya Late Bronze Age Excavation," *National Geographic*, September 21, 2010.

CHAPTER THREE: SHINAN

"These women dive . . . in season.": Chan, Emily, "Invaluable Life Lessons From the 60-Plus 'Sea Women' Of South Korea Who Harvest The Ocean By Hand," *British Vogue*, June 8, 2020.

"When you are . . . [than that]": Chan, Emily, "Invaluable Life Lessons From the 60-Plus 'Sea Women' Of South Korea Who Harvest The Ocean By Hand."

"I can make . . . haenyeo proudly.": Chan, Emily, "Invaluable Life Lessons From the 60-Plus 'Sea Women' Of South Korea Who Harvest The Ocean By Hand."

"the richest ancient . . . ever discovered.": Chang, Kyung-Ho, "The Shinan Shipwreck," *International Seminar on the Korean Culture and the Silk Roads,* February 1991.

"It must have . . . the time.": Woo-young, Lee, "Treasures from Sinan shipwreck on view," *Korean Herald,* July 6, 2016.

CHAPTER FOUR: THE MARY ROSE

"His majesty is . . . accomplished prince.": McKee, Alexander, *How We Found the Mary Rose,* 1982.

"Earth was misnamed . . . beyond words.": Ibid.

"Even in the . . . so long.": Quoted in Blot, *Underwater Archaeology.*

"The *Mary Rose* . . . actually was.": McKee, Alexander, *How We Found the Mary Rose.*

"if we find . . . Not if, WHEN.": Ibid.

"We never expected . . . so rich.": Morris, Steven, "Mary Rose ship had multi-ethnic crew, study shows," *Guardian*, May 5, 2021.

"Originally thought . . . a good job.": "The Ship's Dog," Mary Rose Trust, maryrose.org/life-on-board/.

"It was like . . . never know.": Williams, Eleanor, "The Mary Rose: A Tudor ship's secrets revealed," BBC News, May 30, 2013.

"An unforgettable crunch . . . the barqe.": Rule, Margaret, *The Mary Rose: The Excavation and Raising of Henry VIII's flagship.* "About," maryroseorg.

"Request permission . . . of 437 years.": Childs, David, *The Warship Mary Rose: The Life & Times of King Henry VIII's Flagship.*

CHAPTER FIVE: SÃO JOSÉ PAQUETE DE AFRICA

"There had been . . . our field.": Neely, Paula, "The Stories of the Slave Wrecks," *American Archaeology Magazine*, December 20, 2020.

"There was not . . . and another.": Ruane, Michael E, "Haunting relics from a slave ship headed for African American museum," *Washington Post*, July 16, 2016.

"When I looked . . . long hair.": *The Interesting Narrative of the Life of Olaudah Equiano, or Gustavus Vassa, The African.* London, 1789.

"It's like diving . . . ever worked on.": Ingeno, Lauren, "Archaeologist Resurfaces Stories from a Sunken Slave Ship," Phys.org, June 10, 2015.

"It's a pretty . . . as well.": Catlin, Roger, "Smithsonian to Receive Artifacts from Sunken 18th-Century Slave Ship," *Smithsonian* magazine, May 31, 2015.

"Do something . . . well.": Davis, Rebecca, "Of Sunken Ships and neo-imperialism," *Daily Maverick*, June 3, 2015.

"That constant churning . . . lost to history.": Ibid.

"When we are . . . is told.": Haigler, quoted in "Salvaging Another Piece of Black History," *Harvard Gazette*, October 21, 2020.

"No one is . . . into nothing.": Adams, Kelsey, "'This is a grave site': Diving with a Purpose surfaces the history of the transatlantic slave trade," CBC Radio Canada online, October 18, 2020.

"It was almost . . . very moving.": Ibid.

"I've seen grown . . . your ancestors.": Bruce, Matt, "'Like Touching the Souls of Your Ancestors': Team of Black Scuba Divers Share Experience of Salvaging Sunken Slave Ships," *Atlanta Black Star*, November 26, 2020.

"The story of . . . we live.": van Niekerk, Piet and Werner Hoffman, "Cape Town's slave ship secret," BBC Travel, October 23, 2018.

"Our work . . . and ourselves.": Catlin, Roger, "Smithsonian to Receive Artifacts from Sunken 18th-Century Slave Ship," *Smithsonian* magazine, May 31, 2015.

"And it's not . . . of depravity.": van Niekerk, Piet and Werner Hoffman, "Cape Town's slave ship secret," BBC Travel, October 23, 2018.

CHAPTER SIX: THE *HUNLEY*

"Preserving our maritime . . . shipwreck artifacts.": Mission Statement of the National Underwater and Maritime Agency, numa.net/about-numa-2/.

"[Clive Cussler] . . . find the Hunley.": Butler, quoted in "A Grateful World Says Goodbye to Clive Cussler," Friends of the Hunley, October 5, 2020.

"I have never . . . lost shipwreck.": Cussler, Clive, "Expeditions," National Underwater and Maritime Agency, Mission Statement of the National Underwater and Maritime Agency, numa.net/about-numa-2/.

"It's like unwrapping . . . years now.": Smith, Burce, "After 150 years, Confederate Submarine's Hull Revealed," *Citizen-Times* [Asheville, NC], January 30, 2015.

"All the physical . . . of air.": Lance, quoted in "Duke Grad Student Researches How Confederate Sub Crew Died," Associated Press, August 24, 2017.

"This is the . . . hundred years.": Bates, Karl Leif, "Confederate Submarine Crew Killed by Their Own Weapon," *Duke Today*, August 23, 2017.

CHAPTER SEVEN: THE *EREBUS* AND THE *TERROR*

"There appears to . . . with success.": Sandler, Martin, *Resolute.*

"One would fancy . . . his departure.": Ibid.

"Expectation darkened into . . . into dread.": Ibid.

"I first started . . . never found.": "Historical Tug of War: The Ever-Changing Narrative of the Lost Franklin Expedition," *Canadian Press*, September 16, 2017.

"If it was . . . to listen.": Gaul, Ashleigh, "If any living Inuk knew," *Up Here,* December 2014.

"Louie was someone . . . two ships.": "Inuit Oral Historian Who Pointed Way to Franklin Shipwrecks Dies Aged 58," *Guardian*, March 29, 2018.

"The wreck . . . probably float.": "What Really Happened to HMS Terror? The True Story Behind the Chilling Drama," BT TV, February 26, 2021.

"The technologies . . . a particular time.":Davison, Janis, "What Lies Beneath," CBC Radio-Canada, cbc.ca/news2/interactives/sh/tixaWyQzFX/what-lies-beneath.

"Our goal is . . . of history.": Woods, Allan, "Saga of the Northwest Passage," *Archaeology* magazine, March/April 2012.

FOR FURTHER EXPLORATION

"It's like another . . . in time.": "Shipwreck found in Black Sea is 'world's oldest intact,'" *BBC News*, October 23, 2018.

"A ship surviving . . . in the ancient world.": Rawlinson, Kevin, "World's oldest intact shipwreck discovered in Black Sea," *Guardian,* October 22, 2018.

"There is glass.": Lawton, John, "Shards of History," *Aramco World*, July/August 1984.

"We saw . . . in the world.": Bass, George, *Archaeology Beneath the Sea*, 1976.

"This was a shipwreck . . . Byzantine Empire.": Throckmorton, Peter, *The Lost Ships*, 1964.

"In the world . . . seek freedom.": Natasha, P, "Archeologists against treasure hunters of a shipwreck off Florida's Coast Pits," *Histecho*, April 1, 2020.

"We don't want . . . understanding.": Ibid.

"The discovery of . . . impossible.": Loffhagen, Emma, "Endurance: Who was Ernest Shackleton, what is the history of the ship and why is the discovery so important?" *Evening Standard*, March 10, 2022.

SELECTED BIBLIOGRAPHY

Bass, George. *Archaeology Beneath the Sea.* New York: Harper, 1976.

Bass, George F., ed. *Beneath the Seven Seas: Adventures with the Institute of Nautical Archaeology.* London: Thames & Hudson Ltd., 2005.

Blot, Jean-Yves. *Underwater Archaeology: Exploring the World Beneath the Sea.* Eastbourne, England: Gardners Books, 1996.

Boshoff, Jaco Jacques, Lonnie G. Bunch, Paul Gardullo, and Stephen C. Lubkemann. *From No Return: The 221-Year Journey of the Slave Ship São José.* Washington, DC: Smithsonian Books, 2017.

Chaffin, Tom. *The H. L. Hunley: The Secret Hope of the Confederacy.* New York: Hill & Wang, 2010.

Jones, Alexander. *A Portable Cosmos: Revealing the Antikythera Mechanism, Scientific Wonder of the Ancient World.* New York: Oxford University Press, 2017.

Marchant, Jo. *Decoding the Heavens: A 2,000-Year-Old Computer—And the Century-Long Search to Discover Its Secrets.* Boston: Da Capo Press, 2009.

Marx, Robert, and Jennifer Marx. *Treasure Lost at Sea: Diving to the World's Great Shipwrecks.* Buffalo: Firefly Books, 2004.

McKee, Alexander. *How We Found the Mary Rose.* New York: Souvenir Press, 1982.

Sandler, Martin W. *Resolute: The Epic Search for the Northwest Passage and John Franklin, and the Discovery of the Queen's Ghost Ship.* New York: Sterling, 2006.

Throckmorton, Peter, ed. *The Sea Remembers: Shipwrecks and Archaeology.* New York: Weidenfeld & Nicolson, 1987.

Underwater Archaeology in Korea. Seoul: National Research Institute of Maritime Cultural Heritage, 2016.

INDEX

IMAGE CREDITS

Diving with a Purpose/Brett Seymour of the Submerged Resource Center, National Park Service: 2-3, 80

Flickr: The Antikythera Shipwreck by Tilemahos Efthimiadis: adapted on 12-13, 17, and 18; Dancing by Tilemahos Efthimiadis: 14; The Antikythera Mechanism by Tilemahos Efthimiadis: 22; Sinan Shipwreck Exhibition 10 by National Museum of Korea: 46; Sinan Shipwreck Exhibition 13 by National Museum of Korea: 59; Sinan Shipwreck Exhibition 04 by National Museum of Korea: 58

Gary Todd/WorldHistoryPics.com: 10, 50, 57

Institute of Nautical Technology: 30, 33, 34, 36, 37, 39, 40, 42

Library of Congress, Prints & Photographs Division, LC-USZ62-44000: 82; LC-USZ62-106828: 86; LC-USZ62-110384: 101

The Mary Rose Trust: 71, 72, 73, 75, 76, 77, 78

Metropolitan Museum of Art, Chinese Junk by Utagawa Yoshitora: 51

Mike Walker/ Alamy Stock Photo: 70

Naval History and Heritage Command, NH 58769: 93; NH 53573: 95; NH 97357-28-KN: 98

Parks Canada, EPA: 115

U.S. Air Force/Tech. Sgt. Hank Hoegen: 97

US Navy, O-0000X-001: 102 (top); 030221-O-0000O-002: 103 (top); 030221-O-0000O-001: 103 (bottom); 030307-N-0000X-002: 104

U.S. National Park Service/Susanna Pershem: 88

Wikimedia commons, Manual 2021 by Xmoussas: 23; A Model of the Cosmos in the ancient Greek Antikythera Mechanism by Freeth, T., Higgon, D., Dacanalis, A. et al.: 24; Antikythera mechanism frontview by Gts-tg: 25; Reconstructed Ship by Garycycles: 49; Hanyeo women by Idobi: 52; Portrait of Henry VIII: 60; Battle of the Solent: 62; Sir George Carew: 63; Battle of Sluys: 64; Bronze Demi Cannon Culverins by The Land: 72; Cape Town from Table Bay: 85; Shackle at the Museum in Chateau de Ducs by Jjher7030: 87; Submarine Torpedo Boat *H.L. Hunley*, Dec. 6, 1863 by Conrad Wise Chapman: 92; *H.L. Hunley* in sodium hydroxide bath by Pi3.124: 99; Commander James Clark Ross by John R. Wildman: 106; HMS *Erebus* and HMS *Terror* in the Antarctic, by James Wilson Carmichael: 107; Elisha Kent Kane engraving by D. G. Thompson: 111; An SSS-100k or 600k Side Scan Sonar by Roy Kabanlit: 112; HMS *Erebus* in the Ice: 113

144